Atlas of the
Biodiversity of California

State of California
The Resources Agency
Department of Fish and Game

CALIFORNIA DEPARTMENT OF FISH AND GAME

Printed in the United States of America.

ISBN: 0-9722291-0-8

Cover design: Dugald Stermer

Title page illustration: Giant redwood (*Sequoiadendron giganteum*)

Back cover photo © Siegfried Matull

State of California
The Resources Agency
Department of Fish and Game

Gray Davis, Governor

Mary D. Nichols,
Secretary of Resources

Robert C. Hight,
Department of Fish and Game
Director

Ronald D. Rempel,
Department of Fish and Game
Deputy Director, Habitat Conservation
Division

Thomas Lupo,
Department of Fish and Game
Branch Chief, Wildlife and Habitat
Data Analysis Branch

Project Manager/Cartographer
Eric Kauffman

Editor
Monica Parisi

Photo Editor
Diana Hickson

Layout and Graphic Artist
Joseph Vondracek

Project Sponsors
Diana Jacobs
Ronald Rempel
Sonke Mastrup
Thomas Lupo
Joseph Carboni
Janine Salwasser

Message from the Director

It is with a great deal of pride that the California Department of Fish and Game presents this Atlas of the Biodiversity of California.

Those of us who live in California know that it is an amazing place, and one of the reasons our state is so unique is the incredible diversity of life throughout its length and breadth. This extraordinary biodiversity provides both ecological and aesthetic benefits to the people who live in and visit our state. Everything from recreation to California's economy is enhanced by the variety of animal and plant resources found in every corner of the Golden State.

The Department's formal mission statement is "to manage California's diverse fish, wildlife, and plant resources, and the habitats upon which they depend, for their ecological values and for their use and enjoyment by the public." To successfully realize this mission, we must know what those resources are and where to find them. This atlas is a major step toward bringing all that we do know together in one place. As the Department continues and expands its use of science as a critical tool in developing and making natural resource policies in the state, having easy access to information such as that contained in this book is invaluable to all of us.

Robert C. Hight

Robert C. Hight
Director, California Department of Fish and Game

Acknowledgments

We gratefully acknowledge the many individuals who helped make this book a reality. Its authors, who are all from the California Department of Fish and Game, along with the many others who lent their time and expertise to this project, are listed below. Our gratitude extends to all staff in both the Department's Wildlife and Habitat Data Analysis Branch and the Geographic Information System Service Unit of the Information Technology Branch for their support. We would also like to thank Janine Salwasser, who first shared her vision for a biodiversity atlas during her 1998-2000 tenure as Chief of the Wildlife and Habitat Data Analysis Branch. The California Wildlife Foundation and its Board of Directors and The Nature Conservancy generously provided additional funding for this project. We especially thank the authors and editors of the book, *Precious Heritage: The Status of Biodiversity in the United States* (Stein et al. 2000), whose work inspired us to create an atlas of the biodiversity of California.

Concept and Storyboard
Eva Begley
Roxanne Bittman
Joseph Carboni
Scott Collier
Jack Edwards
Patrick Gaul
Barrett Garrison
Robert Garrison
Gregory Greenwood
Patricia Hernandez
Diana Hickson
Marc Hoshovsky
Paul Ideker
Diana Jacobs
Eric Kauffman
Todd Keeler-Wolf
Lora Konde
Sara Lee
Eric Loft
Thomas Lupo
Terry Mansfield
Jenny Marr
Sonke Mastrup
Darlene McGriff
Anne Milliken
Sandra Morey
Monica Parisi
Ronald Rempel
Alexia Retallack
Ronald Rogers
Janine Salwasser
Kevin Shaffer
Kent Smith
Chris Stermer
Craig Turner

Authorship
Helen Birss
Roxanne Bittman
Esther Burkett
Scott Clemons
Larry Espinosa
Barrett Garrison
Diana Hickson

Kathy Hieb
Kathy Hill
Marc Hoshovsky
Kevin Hunting
Diana Jacobs
Ron Jurek
Eric Kauffman
Todd Keeler-Wolf
Chuck Knutson
Kari Lewis
Eric Loft
Darlene McGriff
Becky Miller
Monica Parisi
Steve Parmenter
Joe Pisciotto
Gail Presley
Ronald Rempel
Ronald Rogers
Janine Salwasser
Melanie Weaver

Manuscript and Data Review
Bruce Baldwin
Roxanne Bittman
Betsy Bolster
Dirk Brazil
Ann Chrisney
Scott Clemons
Jim Cole
Josh Collins
Richard Erickson
Sam Fitton
Scott Flint
Lawrence Fox III
John Gendron
Thomas Hickson
Robert Hight
Marc Hoshovsky
Ann Howald
Paul Ideker
Diana Jacobs
Sharon Keeney
Todd Keeler-Wolf

Thomas King
Mary Larson
William Laudenslayer, Jr.
Cynthia LeDoux-Bloom
Jeff Lewis
Alice Low
Thomas Lupo
Dean Marston
Sonke Mastrup
Dennis McEwan
Robert Mesta
Richard Moe
Peter Moyle
John Nelson
Gail Newton
Steve Newton-Reed
Ruth Ostroff
Peter Perrine
Ed Pert
Joe Pisciotto
Michael Pitcairn
Tim Ramirez
Ronald Rempel
Alexia Retallack
Ronald Rogers
Glen Rollins
John Sawyer
Carey Smith
William Somer
Richard Standiford
Bruce Stein
Bill Stewart
David Tibor
Bonnie Turner
Dee Warenycia
Kim Webb
Larry Week
Hartwell Welsh, Jr.
Nancy Wright
Dan Yparraguirre
Cynthia Zabel
William Zielinski

Data Analysis Consultation and Support
Richard Baron
Robin Carlson
Scott Collier
Jerry Davis
Kristi Fien
Patricia Hernandez
Lora Konde
Ann Mahaney
Fiona McNeill
Will Patterson
Shawn Saving
Chris Stermer
Steve Torres
Craig Turner
Mehrey Vaghti

Photography
Bill Basom
Caitlin Bean
Roxanne Bittman
Betsy Bolster
Joseph Carboni
N.H. (Dan) Cheatham
Bob Corey
Buff Corsi
Gerald Corsi
Willy Cowell
Ed Ely
Julie Evens
Dennis Flaherty
Timothy Floyd
James Gallagher
John Game
Daniel W. Gotshall
Brenda Grewell
Bill Hamilton
John Hannon
Douglas Herr
Marc Hoshovsky
Ken Howard
Diana Jacobs
Les Junge

Todd Keeler-Wolf
Russ Kerr
Tom King
Peter L. Knapp
Fritz Knopf
Frank Kratofil
Siegfried Matull
Karen McClymonds
Darlene McGriff
Curtis Milliron
Don Moore
John C. Muegge
Barbara J. Nelson
Brian O'Neill
Bill Palmer
B. Moose Peterson
Phil Pister
Allan Renger
Peter Rissler
Galen Rowell
Sherburn R. Sanborn
Larry Serpa
Hugh P. Smith, Jr.
Thomas Taylor
Rodney Temples
Susan Van Der Wal
David Welling
Carol W. Witham
Karen Wyatt

Graphic Design and Layout Consultation
Jeanne Gunther
Kathy Ross

Illustrations
Randy Babb
Kathy Ross
Dugald Stermer

Image Processing
Phillip Deák

About the Artist

Tuctoria mucronata

$\int$ O L A N O G R A $\int$ $\int$

Dugald **Stermer** is a native Californian whose illustrations have appeared in numerous books, magazines, and posters. He is the author of four books: *Vanishing Creatures*, *Vanishing Flora*, *Birds & Bees*, and *The Art of Revolution*. His illustrations span topics from rare plants and animals to human anatomy to political commentary. Mr. Stermer lives in San Francisco, where he is the Chair of the Illustration Department of the California College of Arts and Crafts.

Atlas of the Biodiversity of California

Table of Contents

A Definition of Biodiversity

Erysimum capitatum *var. angustatum*

CONTRA COSTA WALLFLOWER

California: A Definition of Biodiversity

By Janine Salwasser

California is truly a special place for a great variety of plants and animals. Of any state in the United States, California has both the highest total number of species and the highest number of endemic species—those that occur nowhere else. The state is home to several of the nation's biological "hotspots" (see map at right) and is one of the 25 "hotspots" identified worldwide (Stein et al. 2000).

This variety of life, or biodiversity, can be explained by our unique geography and geologic history. Where else can you find the highest point and the lowest point in the contiguous United States? Mount Whitney (14,494 feet) and Badwater, Death Valley (282 feet below sea level) are within 80 miles of each other, and both are only 200 miles from the Pacific Ocean. California's high mountain ranges and deserts have kept native animals and plants relatively isolated from the rest of the continent. The warm summers and mild winters of California's rare Mediterranean climate also make the habitats different from other parts of the country. Then there is the sheer size of the state; California is more than 100 million acres in area. Add these factors together and you have one of the planet's richest places for plant and animal diversity.

Because California is also a great place for human life, it is home to the largest population of people in the country, with the highest projected growth rates into the future. The human demands for the land, water, and natural resources that make life so abundant in California present the greatest threats to its unique plants and animals. California leads the nation in number of rare species within a state, and nearly one third of its species are identified as at risk in the United States. Our challenge is to meet the needs of society while maintaining the state's remarkable biodiversity for future generations.

Endemism Ranks for California in the United States	Number of Endemics in California	Rank Among U.S. States (Stein et al. 2000)
Vascular Plant Taxa (species, subspecies, and varieties)	2,153	1
Amphibian Species	17	1
Reptile Species	5	1
Bird Species	2	2
Mammal Species	17	1
Freshwater Fish Species	20	1

Richness in California and the United States	Total Number in California (Jepson Flora Project 2002, CDFG and CIWTG 2002, Moyle and Davis 2000)	Total Number in the United States (Stein et al. 2000)	Percent of United States Total in California
Vascular Plant Taxa (species, subspecies, and varieties)	6,272		
Vascular Plant Species	5,047	15,890	32%
Amphibian Species	51	231	22%
Reptile Species	84	283	30%
Bird Species (regularly-occurring)	433	768	56%
Mammal Species	197	416	47%
Freshwater Fish Species	67	799	8%

Total Biodiversity Ranks for California Among U.S. States (Stein et al. 2000)	
Richness	1
Rarity (% At Risk)	2
Endemism	1

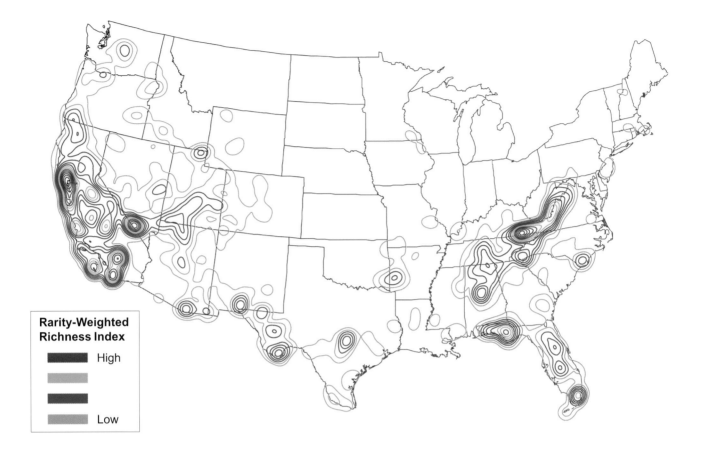

Rarity-Weighted Richness Index

High

Low

Rarity and Richness Hotspots in the United States
(See page 7 for explanation of Rarity-Weighted Richness Index.)
Source: *Precious Heritage*, Stein et al. 2000. Used by permission.

Special Status Taxa in California (As defined in Glossary. Source: California Department of Fish and Game 2003a)	
Plants	2,089
Amphibians	39
Reptiles	42
Birds	135
Mammals	120
Freshwater Fishes	90
Total	2,515

Percentage of United States At Risk Species Found in California (Defined as Ranks GX to G3 in Stein et al. 2000)		
Plants	32%	(1,699/5,244)
Amphibians	23%	(19/84)
Reptiles	29%	(15/51)
Birds	19%	(20/108)
Mammals	41%	(27/66)
Freshwater Fishes	10%	(30/300)
Total	31%	(1,810/5,853)

Rarity in California and the United States

An Introduction to the Atlas

By Monica Parisi

Working Definition of Biodiversity

Biodiversity may be defined on many different levels. For a regional landscape or an entire state, it is the diversity of species, habitats, and vegetation types. For a habitat or vegetation type, it is the diversity of life forms within it. For a species, it is the genetic variation within a population or among populations.

For the purposes of this atlas, we are examining biodiversity on a statewide level. This atlas presents a summary of the best available information we have to date on species, habitats, and vegetation types at that level. A complete analysis of biodiversity would include many groups of living things for which we lack statewide data. This would include fungi, lichens, most non-vascular plants, such as mosses, and more. For animals, this would include most invertebrates, such as mollusks, insects, spiders, and crustaceans. Also, the distributions of many marine fishes are just now being mapped for the waters off California's coast.

However, we can still begin to identify places on the landscape where biodiversity appears to be unusually high. The main components of our analyses are presented below:

Richness —a measure of diversity—is the total number of plant taxa, animal species, or vegetation types in a given area. Note that this is the number of species or taxa, rather than the number of individuals. An area high in bird richness, for example, supports many different species of birds. The density of birds is not necessarily higher here than in other areas of the state.

Rarity —a measure of sensitivity—is used for those taxa that have special status due to very limited distribution, low population levels, or immediate threat, such as habitat conversion. An area high in rarity has many taxa that meet this definition.

Endemism —a measure of natural distribution—is used for those taxa that are found only in one specific area, such as one region or the state itself. A region of high endemism has many taxa restricted to it.

Organization of the Atlas

Most of the biological data presented in this atlas are in two major sections. The first is "Measures of Biodiversity: Richness, Rarity, and Endemism." Except for the map showing richness of vegetation types, every map in this section represents a statewide analysis of richness or rarity for a major taxonomic group such as plants, mammals, or invertebrates. The methods used to create these maps are presented below. The second major section is "Samples of Biodiversity: Habitats and Species from Throughout California." The maps in this section represent the distribution of specific habitats or species across one or more regions of the state and are therefore organized roughly by region. The 10 regions shown in outline over each statewide map are the bioregions adopted by the California Biodiversity Council. The regions are described throughout the richness accounts.

The symbols and data layers common to all of the maps in this atlas are presented on page 8. Readers should also note that there is a glossary of biological, geographical, and management terms beginning on page 93.

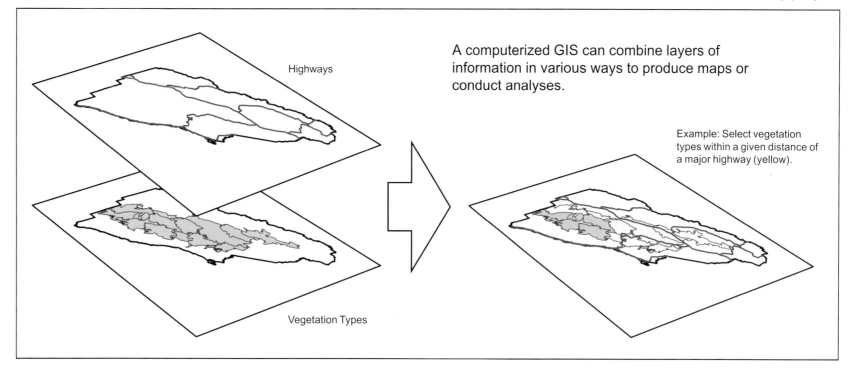

Highways

A computerized GIS can combine layers of information in various ways to produce maps or conduct analyses.

Example: Select vegetation types within a given distance of a major highway (yellow).

Vegetation Types

What a Computerized Geographic Information System (GIS) Can Do

Creation of the Maps—A Technical Description

All of the maps in this atlas were created using a geographic information system (GIS). A GIS may be thought of as an organized assemblage of people, data, techniques, computers, and programs for acquiring, analyzing, storing, retrieving, and displaying spatial information about the real world. A computerized GIS is an excellent tool for representing the real world because it can easily combine layers of information in various ways to conduct analyses and create maps (see figure above).

Richness Maps

Maps showing richness of vegetation types, plant taxa, and animal species were each created using a slightly different set of techniques. This is largely because not all biological data have been collected using the same geographic references.

The map showing richness of vegetation types was created from a database of plant alliances known to occur in each of 220 ecological subsections as defined by the United States Forest Service (Miles and Goudey 1997). Not all of the approximately 400 plant alliances have been mapped in detail throughout the state, but all are known to the level of precision afforded by the ecological subsections. The subsections represent a division of the state based on geographic variables relevant to vegetation such as climate, topography, and soil type.

The map of plant richness comes from data provided by the Jepson Flora Project of the Jepson Herbarium, which is housed at the University of California, Berkeley and is devoted exclusively to the study of California's native plants. The data were derived from *The Jepson Manual: Higher Plants of California* (Hickman 1993), in which each species, subspecies, or variety of plant is reported to occur in one or more geographic subdivisions. These subdivisions are hierarchical, with the entire state represented as "CA" and three provinces within it represented as "GB" for Great Basin, "D" for Desert, and "CA-FP" for the California Floristic Province, which includes the Sierra Nevada and everything to the west, and the Transverse Ranges and everything to the south. Smaller subregions nest within each of these three provinces. The largest subdivision that accurately represents the perceived distribution of a plant was used to produce the dataset and the richness map. For example, a plant in the manual with a distribution described as "CA-FP" was assigned to all of the subregions west of the Sierra and south of the Transverse Ranges.

For vertebrates, richness maps representing amphibians, reptiles, birds, and mammals were created using range maps from the California Wildlife Habitat Relationships (CWHR) System (CDFG and CIWTG 2002). CWHR is an information system and predictive model for California's wildlife containing range maps and habitat relationships information on all of the

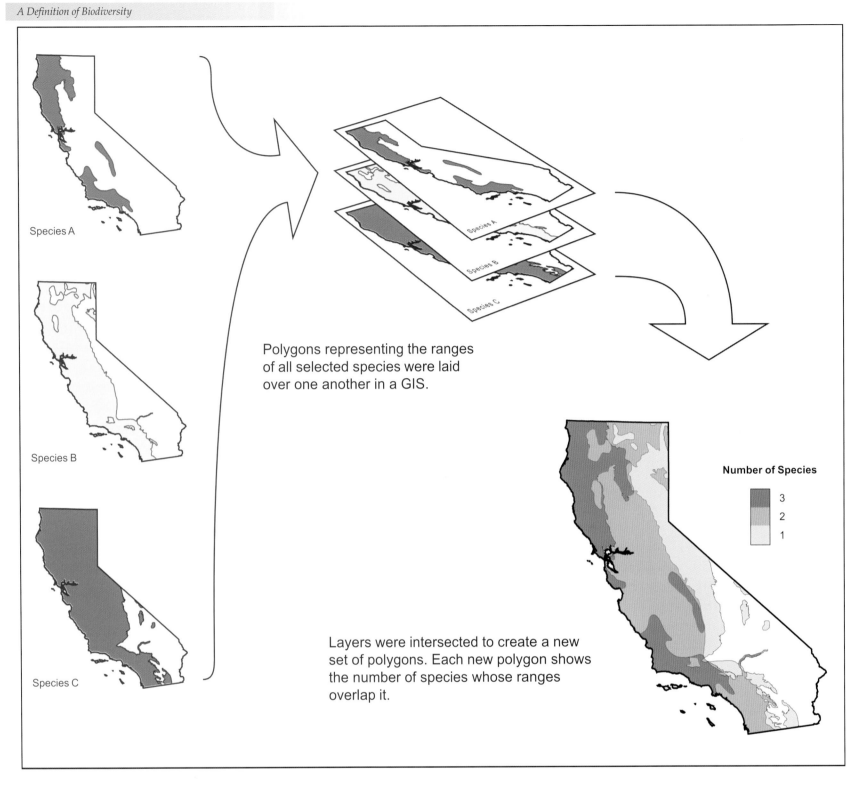

Polygons representing the ranges of all selected species were laid over one another in a GIS.

Layers were intersected to create a new set of polygons. Each new polygon shows the number of species whose ranges overlap it.

Species A

Species B

Species C

Number of Species

3
2
1

How Richness Maps for Amphibians, Reptiles, Birds, Mammals, and Freshwater Fishes Were Created

state's regularly-occurring terrestrial vertebrate species. Range maps from CWHR represent the current maximum geographic extent of species within California. Suitable habitat for a species may or may not be present at any given location within the depicted range. Fish range maps were provided by Peter Moyle and Paul Randall of the University of California, Davis Department of Wildlife and Fisheries Conservation Biology, who developed them in cooperation with several state agencies and The Nature Conservancy (Moyle et al. 1998).

For each animal richness map, polygons representing the ranges of all selected species were laid over one another in a GIS and intersected to create a new set of polygons (see figure above). We then determined the total number of species whose ranges were represented by the new polygons. Except where noted, we created the classes shown on the legend by looking for natural breaks in a frequency distribution of the number of polygons sharing similar values. The richness maps for all animals are presented at the species level.

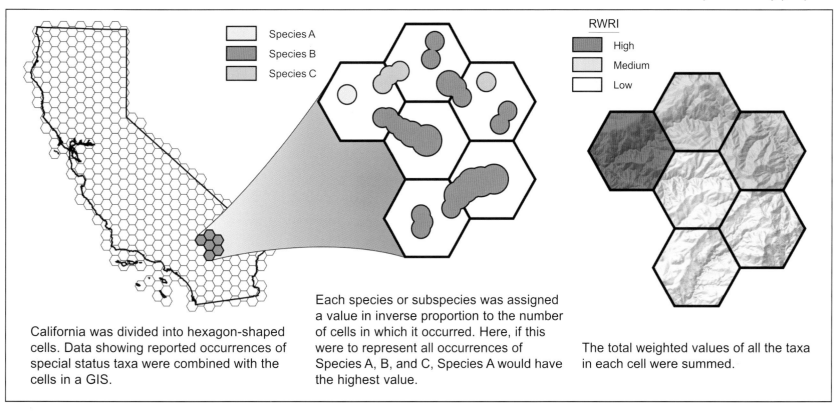

California was divided into hexagon-shaped cells. Data showing reported occurrences of special status taxa were combined with the cells in a GIS.

Each species or subspecies was assigned a value in inverse proportion to the number of cells in which it occurred. Here, if this were to represent all occurrences of Species A, B, and C, Species A would have the highest value.

The total weighted values of all the taxa in each cell were summed.

How Rarity Maps Were Created

Rarity Maps

Maps representing high priority special status plants and animals, including fish and invertebrates, were created using occurrence data from the California Natural Diversity Database (CNDDB) (CDFG 2003a). CNDDB is a statewide inventory of the locations and conditions of the state's rarest plant and animal species and vegetation types. CNDDB is California's natural heritage program and is part of NatureServe's Natural Heritage Network, a nationwide network of similar programs started by The Nature Conservancy.

A "rarity-weighted richness index" (RWRI) was used as the measure of rarity. The Association for Biodiversity Information, now known as NatureServe, used this approach in a nationwide analysis of "rarity hotspots" using natural heritage program data from all 50 states (Stein et al. 2000). As in their analysis, we used the United States Environmental Protection Agency's Environmental Monitoring and Assessment Program (EMAP) grid system to divide the state into hexagonal grid cells of 250.4 square miles each (Spence and White 1992, White et al. 1992).

The RWRI takes into account not only the richness of special status taxa within a cell but the relative rarity of each of those taxa or elements. Each element—which may be a species, subspecies, variety, or "evolutionarily significant unit" (ESU)—in a hexagon is assigned a weight based on the inverse of the

number of hexagons in which it occurs. An element is only counted once in any given cell, regardless of the number of occurrences of that element in that cell. Elements with the highest weights are those that occur in the fewest number of cells; their distributions are the most limited. The weights are then summed for each of the cells. Cells with the highest values represent the highest concentrations of special status taxa that are also the most restricted in terms of where they occur (see figure above).

Such an index has also been characterized as an "index of irreplaceability" because cells with the highest values are, theoretically, the most irreplaceable and thus have the highest significance for the conservation of biodiversity. Use of the index for conservation rests on several assumptions, one being that the entire distribution of any given special status element in California is known. This means that all potential habitat for a species or subspecies has been systematically surveyed and that all known occurrences have been reported to CNDDB, which is not necessarily the case. Also, for any given species or subspecies, an analysis of irreplaceability might also include such factors as total population size and reproductive success—data only available for a few species in selected areas of the state. Nonetheless, the RWRI serves as a strong indicator of irreplaceability.

About the Maps

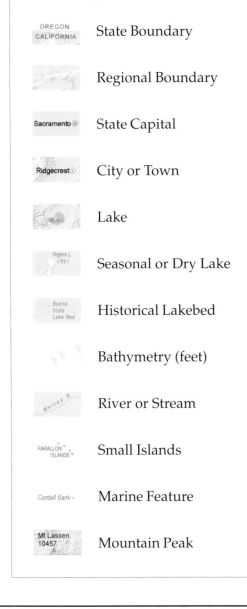

Map Symbols

   These map symbols appear on most of the maps in this atlas. Unique symbolism is explained in the legend for each map.

OREGON / CALIFORNIA	State Boundary
	Regional Boundary
Sacramento	State Capital
Ridgecrest	City or Town
Mono L.	Lake
Rogers L. (dry)	Seasonal or Dry Lake
Buena Vista Lake Bed	Historical Lakebed
	Bathymetry (feet)
Merced R.	River or Stream
FARALLON ISLANDS	Small Islands
Cordell Bank	Marine Feature
Mt Lassen 10457	Mountain Peak

Notes on reading the maps

Longitude tic marks on top and bottom neatlines count from east to west.

Legend describes the information specific to each map.

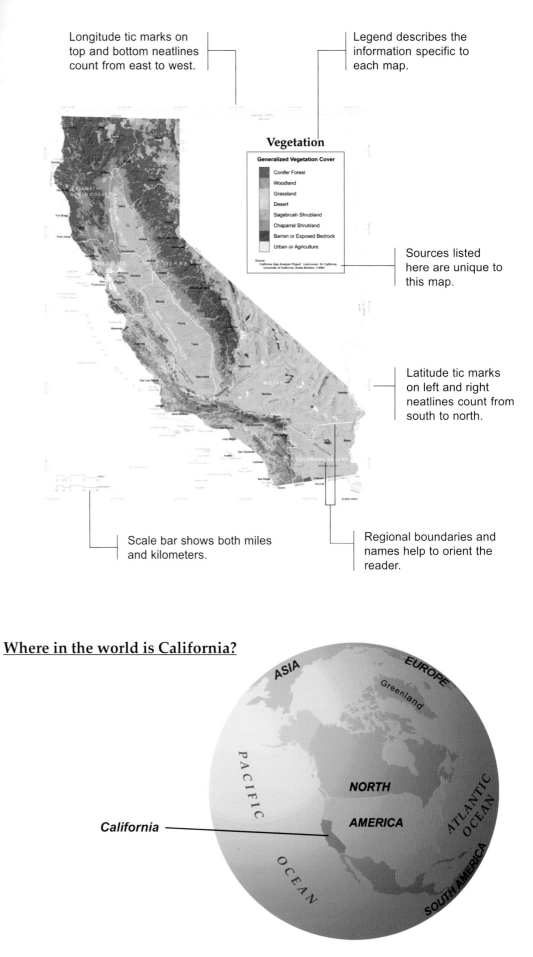

Sources listed here are unique to this map.

Latitude tic marks on left and right neatlines count from south to north.

Scale bar shows both miles and kilometers.

Regional boundaries and names help to orient the reader.

Where in the world is California?

Base Map Data Sources

United States Geological Survey
    State Boundaries
    Capitals and Cities
    Hydrography (lakes, rivers, coastline)
    Place Names
    Digital Elevation Model

National Oceanic and Atmospheric Administration
    Bathymetry
    Marine Place Names

Environmental Systems Research Institute
    State and International Boundaries

California State Lands Commission
    Coastline and Islands

California Biodiversity Council
    Regional Boundaries

Map Projection

All maps created for this atlas use a projection called "California Albers," which was originally developed in the early 1990s by the GIS staff at the Stephen P. Teale Data Center (State of California). This projection was selected because it does a relatively good job of depicting California on a flat surface. The parameters of this projection are listed below.

Projection Name:	California Albers
Type:	Albers Equal Area Conic
Datum:	North American Datum (1927)
Spheroid:	Clark (1866)

Parameters:

Units:	Meters
False Northing:	-4000000 meters
Central Meridian:	-120 00 00 (longitude)
Standard Parallels:	
	34 00 00 (latitude)
	40 30 00 (latitude)
Latitude of Origin:	00 00 00 (Equator)

Notes on Datasets

All maps in the atlas present the most comprehensive statewide or regional datasets available for the topics chosen. To some extent the topics chosen, particularly those biological features highlighted in the section showing sample habitats and species, reflect what datasets were available. Richness and rarity maps in the Measures of Biodiversity section include data for native taxa only. Maps in the Samples of Biodiversity section show current ranges to the best of our knowledge. None of the maps in the atlas include the historical range of a featured element or attempt to compare current with historic information. One of the difficulties in doing this in a computerized GIS is that a great deal of historic data is not yet stored in a computerized format.

Notes on Scientific Names

Names of vascular plants are from *The Jepson Manual: Higher Plants of California* (Hickman 1993). The standard reference for marine algae used here is *Marine Algae of California* (Abbott and Hollenberg 1976). Names of amphibians and reptiles are generally those used by Stebbins (1985) in the second edition of *A Field Guide to Western Reptiles and Amphibians*, although some individual taxonomic changes have been published since then and we have used new names where appropriate. Names of birds are those published in the seventh edition of *The A.O.U. Checklist of North American Birds* (American Ornithologists' Union 1998). We have adopted the scientific convention of capitalizing the official common names of birds from this checklist. Mammal names are from the *Revised Checklist of North American Mammals North of Mexico* (Jones et al. 1997) except where more recent taxonomic changes have been published. Names of fishes are those published by the American Fisheries Society in the fifth edition of *Common and Scientific Names of Fishes from the United States and Canada* (1991). One exception here to the naming conventions used in the 1991 publication is the capitalization of Chinook in the name Chinook salmon, a decision made by the American Fisheries Society Committee on Names of Fishes after publishing the 1991 list. For invertebrate animals, we adopted the names used by NatureServe, whose references by taxonomic group are listed at *www.natureserve.org*.

A Remarkable Geography

To explain California's biodiversity we must first look at its geography. California has an extremely varied topography. Its valleys, mountains, and coastlines are continually being shaped. The landscape has experienced long term climate changes, and each advance and retreat of an ice age resulted in a new mix of species. We can explain much about the biodiversity of the state by looking at its topography, geology, soils, and climate. Vegetation patterns on the landscape reflect this remarkable geography.

Climate and Topography

By Eric Kauffman

California is one of the few places where five major climate types occur in close proximity. Here, the Desert, Cool Interior, Highland, and Steppe climates border a smaller region of Mediterranean climate. Perhaps the only other place like California is central Chile, where this convergence is made even more extreme by the dramatic Andean topography.

As climates go, the Mediterranean climate is rare. Outside of the Mediterranean Sea region, it is limited to five locations: two in Australia, one in South Africa, one in Chile, and one in California.

In California, the Mediterranean climate has three variations. One is the cool summer/cool winter climate found along the coast and the western slope of the Sierra Nevada. A second variation, also along the coast, is similar but has frequent summer fog. The third is an interior valley version with hotter summers and cooler winters. With all types, most of the precipitation falls in winter—not summer—which is unusual for much of the world, where the opposite is true.

The mild temperatures and winter rain of the Mediterranean climate support some of the highest species richness in the state. Interestingly, however, California's Desert climates rival the Mediterranean for plant and animal species richness. For California's deserts, topography comes into play along with climate. The Mojave Region is characterized by sweeping valleys and rugged, high elevation mountain ranges. In general, upper elevations catch more rain and snow, and are much cooler than the valleys below. Nowhere is this more apparent than in the contrast between Death Valley, which is below sea level, and the Panamint Range, with peaks as high as 10,000 feet

above sea level. In Death Valley, plants and animals may bake in 115 degree summer heat while 12 miles away and 2 miles up, cool breezes blow through the dark green needles of bristlecone pine (*Pinus longaeva*) and the delicate leaves of mountain maple (*Acer glabrum*).

California's higher elevations, such as those found in the Modoc and Sierra regions, generally have two major climate types: a Cool Interior climate and a Highland climate. In these areas, the conditions that determine most other climates (latitude, prevailing winds, and temperature) are strongly modified by elevation, slope, and aspect. Aspect, or the direction a slope faces, is very important. South facing slopes catch the sun's rays and heat, making them warmer and drier, while shaded north facing slopes are cooler and wetter. West facing slopes tend to catch more precipitation from storms moving inland from the Pacific Ocean. The result is vegetation diversity—even on a single mountain. For example, a ridge may have oaks and open grass areas on one side and a dense canopy of fir or pine trees on the other.

California's Steppe climate of the San Joaquin Valley Region is hot like a desert, but averages enough moisture to support grasslands and other vegetation not commonly found in the desert.

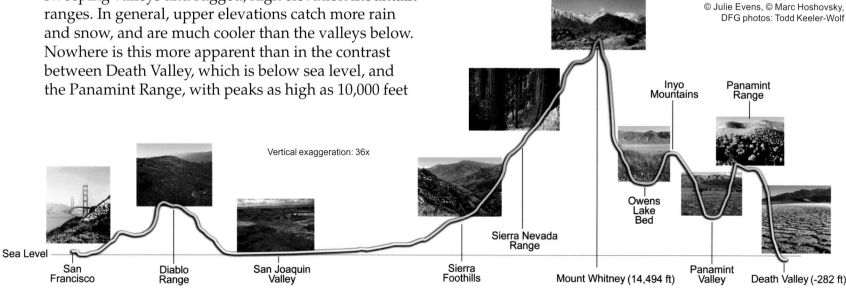

© Julie Evens, © Marc Hoshovsky, DFG photos: Todd Keeler-Wolf

Vertical exaggeration: 36x

Inyo Mountains

Panamint Range

Sierra Nevada Range

Owens Lake Bed

Sea Level

San Francisco

Diablo Range

San Joaquin Valley

Sierra Foothills

Mount Whitney (14,494 ft)

Panamint Valley

Death Valley (-282 ft)

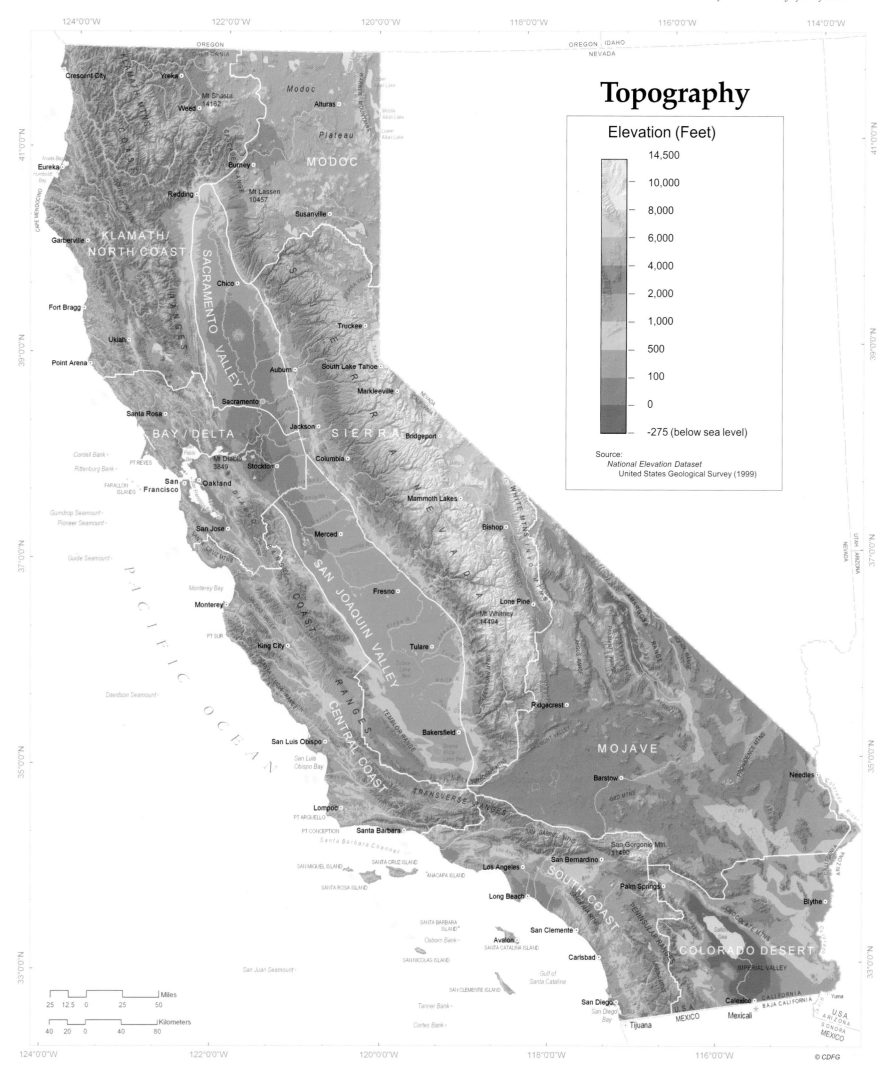

Topography

Elevation (Feet)

- 14,500
- 10,000
- 8,000
- 6,000
- 4,000
- 2,000
- 1,000
- 500
- 100
- 0
- -275 (below sea level)

Source:
National Elevation Dataset
United States Geological Survey (1999)

© CDFG

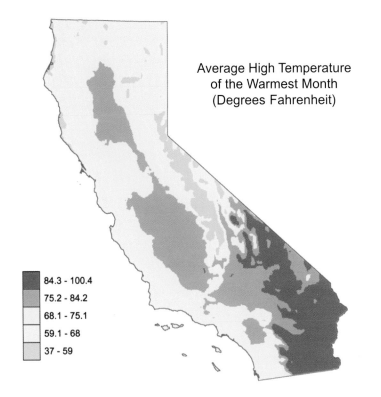

Average High Temperature
of the Warmest Month
(Degrees Fahrenheit)

84.3 - 100.4
75.2 - 84.2
68.1 - 75.1
59.1 - 68
37 - 59

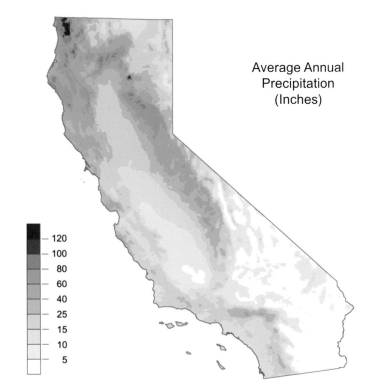

Average Annual
Precipitation
(Inches)

120
100
80
60
40
25
15
10
5

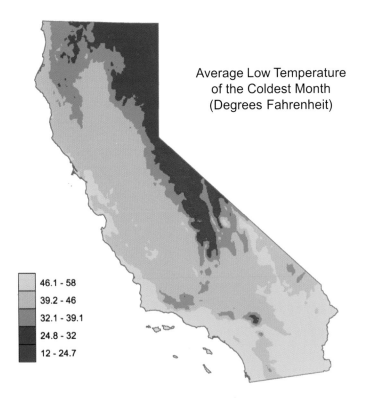

Average Low Temperature
of the Coldest Month
(Degrees Fahrenheit)

46.1 - 58
39.2 - 46
32.1 - 39.1
24.8 - 32
12 - 24.7

Climographs for Selected Climate Stations
(See map on opposite page.)

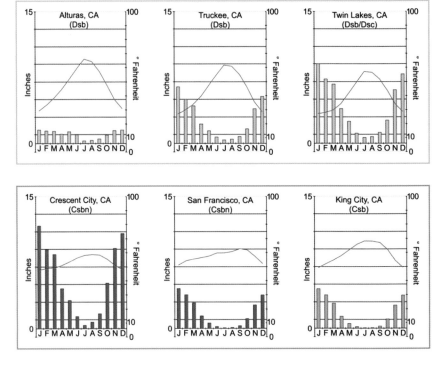

Alturas, CA (Dsb)

Truckee, CA (Dsb)

Twin Lakes, CA (Dsb/Dsc)

Crescent City, CA (Csbn)

San Francisco, CA (Csbn)

King City, CA (Csb)

■ Average Monthly Precipitation (inches)

— Average Monthly Temperature (degrees Fahrenheit)

Sources:
California Average Monthly and Annual Precipitation
California Average Monthly and Annual Temperature
    The Climate Source (1998a and b)
Weather Observation Station Records
    National Climatic Data Center (2002)

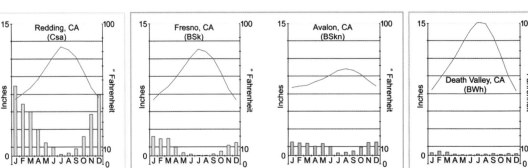

Redding, CA (Csa)

Fresno, CA (BSk)

Avalon, CA (BSkn)

Death Valley, CA (BWh)

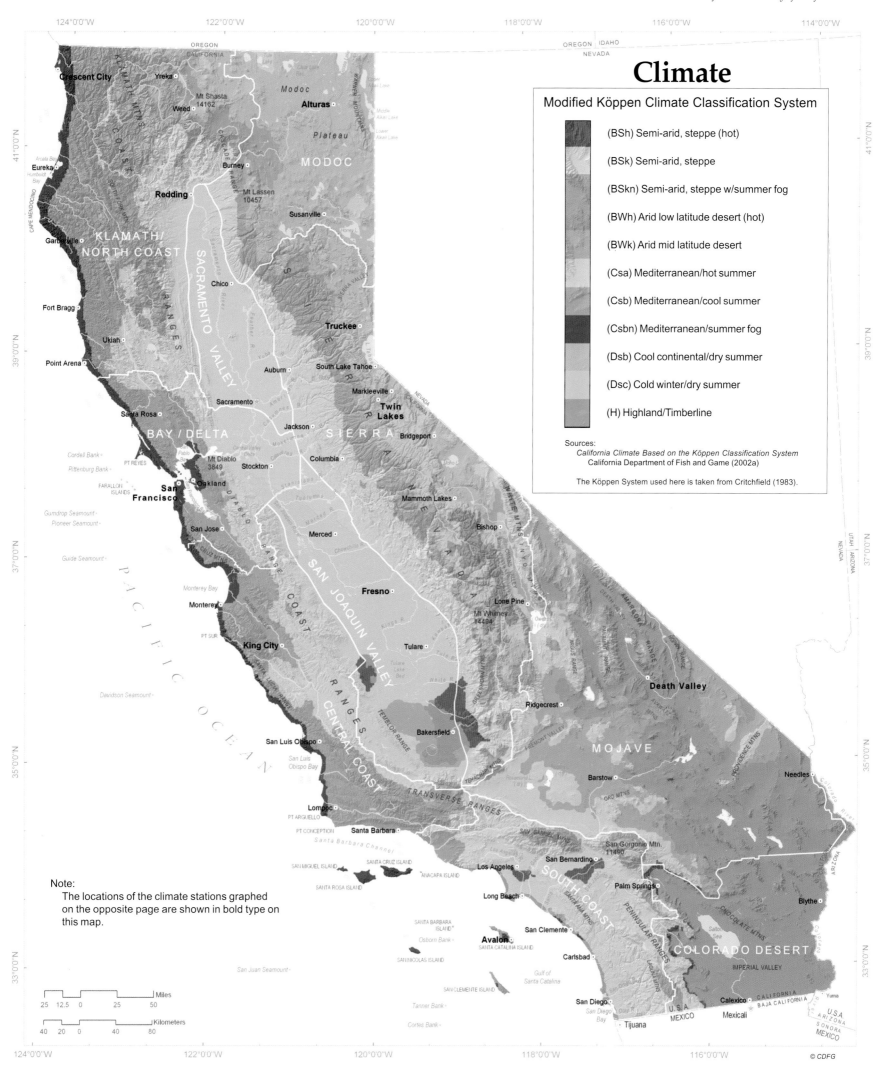

Climate

Modified Köppen Climate Classification System

(BSh) Semi-arid, steppe (hot)

(BSk) Semi-arid, steppe

(BSkn) Semi-arid, steppe w/summer fog

(BWh) Arid low latitude desert (hot)

(BWk) Arid mid latitude desert

(Csa) Mediterranean/hot summer

(Csb) Mediterranean/cool summer

(Csbn) Mediterranean/summer fog

(Dsb) Cool continental/dry summer

(Dsc) Cold winter/dry summer

(H) Highland/Timberline

Sources:
California Climate Based on the Köppen Classification System
California Department of Fish and Game (2002a)

The Köppen System used here is taken from Critchfield (1983).

Note:
The locations of the climate stations graphed on the opposite page are shown in bold type on this map.

© CDFG

Geology and Soils

By Eric Kauffman

The geology of California is both complex and interesting, with active volcanoes, huge granite batholiths, 800 foot deep alluvium, thick limestone and dolomite bedrock, vast areas of serpentine, and much more (Alt and Hyndman 1975, Wright and Pierson 1992, Alt 2000). This breaks down into an equally diverse mix of soils: 10 of the world's 12 soil orders have been mapped in California.

Geology and soil greatly determine the distribution of most plants and the animals that depend on them. This is especially true for plants—some of which have adapted to grow almost exclusively on California's uncommon soils. Soils derived from serpentine are a perfect example. Serpentine forms from peridotite that has undergone intense heat and pressure at a tectonic subduction zone. California is located at the frontier of one of these zones, where an oceanic tectonic plate is being driven under a continental plate. Serpentine rock surfaces at these zones because it is much less dense than surrounding rock (California Department of Conservation 2002).

Trinity Alps, Klamath/North Coast Region
Photo © Marc Hoshovsky

Serpentine soils contain high levels of asbestos, copper, mercury, magnesium, chromium, and other elements, but are low in calcium. Many plants cannot survive in these soils. However, some plants, like the leather oak (*Quercus durata* var. *durata*), not only survive but have evolved to grow almost exclusively on serpentine soils. Because serpentine is not widespread outside of California, many plants that grow in it are also endemic to this state. Approximately 20 percent of the state's rare endemic plants grow on serpentine soils (California Native Plant Society 2001).

Other soils to note are the carbonate types, which come from certain types of bedrock such as limestone, calcareous shale, or dolomite. Like the serpentine endemics, certain plants have evolved to grow in carbonate soils where other plants have difficulty surviving. Other important types of soil are the poorly drained clay soils of the Sacramento and San Joaquin Valley regions, and the mineral rich volcanic soils found in the Modoc Region. Each of these is host to a large number of special status and/or endemic plants.

Coyote Ridge, Bay/Delta Region.
Wildflowers dominate the serpentine soil in the foreground, while introduced grasses thrive in the nutrient-rich soil in the middle distance.
Photo © Julie Evens

Table Mountain, Sacramento Valley Region
Photo © Marc Hoshovsky

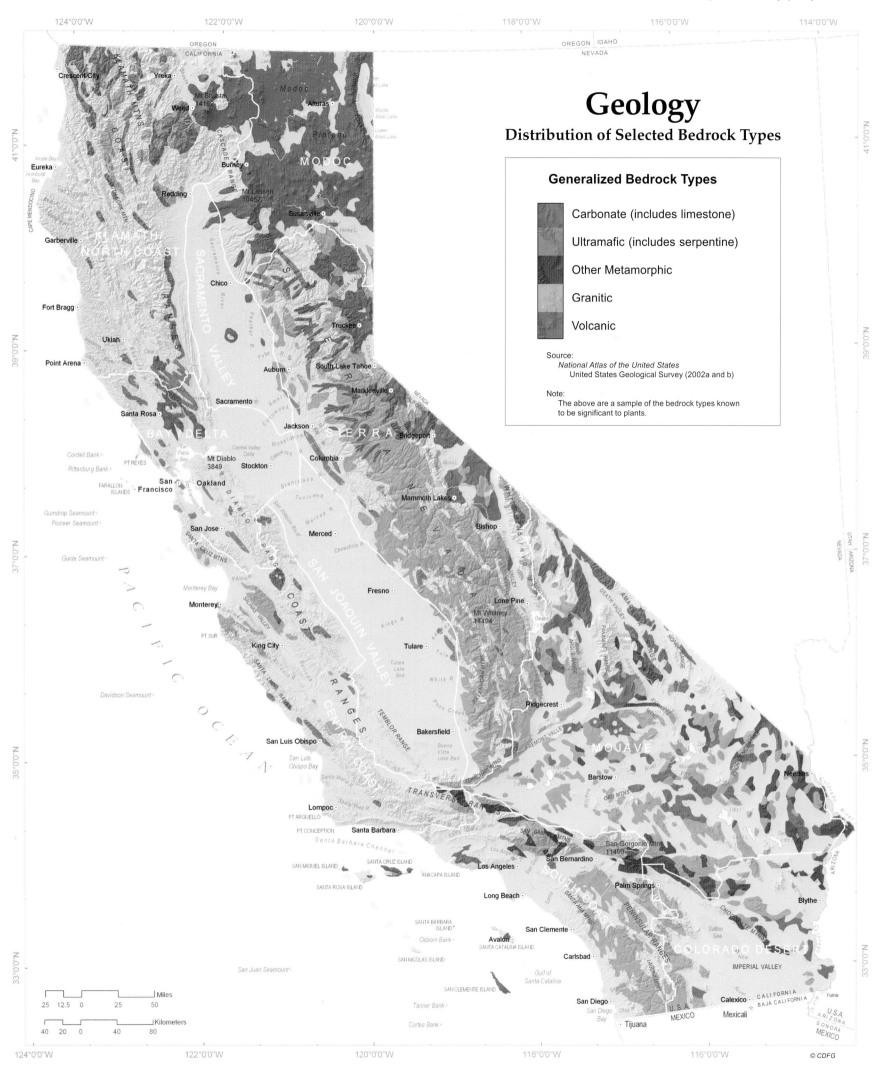

Geology
Distribution of Selected Bedrock Types

Generalized Bedrock Types

Carbonate (includes limestone)

Ultramafic (includes serpentine)

Other Metamorphic

Granitic

Volcanic

Source:
National Atlas of the United States
United States Geological Survey (2002a and b)

Note:
The above are a sample of the bedrock types known
to be significant to plants.

Geography and Vegetation

By Todd Keeler-Wolf

California's diverse geography is reflected in its vegetation. Vegetation expresses the interrelationship between all facets of the physical environment, such as climate and geology, and the primary producers (plants) within that environment. Vegetation may be defined as the patchwork of plant species arrayed across the landscape. It includes a variety of life forms such as trees, shrubs, grasses, forbs, and non-vascular plants like mosses. These different life forms are distributed in different patterns across the land and result in the structure of the vegetation. The individual species of plants within a given patch of vegetation are also characteristic. Thus, vegetation consists of physical life forms and the species of plants that make up those life forms.

Wet meadow complex, Silver King Creek, East Fork Carson River, Sierra Region
Photo © Marc Hoshovsky

The broad patterns of vegetation in the state relate most clearly to the combination of temperature and moisture, which is, in turn, strongly influenced by California's varied topography. (See account entitled "Climate and Topography.") The most extreme climates—the coldest alpine environments and the driest deserts—are largely unvegetated. The cooler and wetter portions of the state are forested with coniferous trees while the drier and hotter portions are unforested and covered with desert scrub. Areas of

Coast sagebrush (*Artemisia californica*) alliance, Garrapata State Park, Central Coast Region
DFG photo: Todd Keeler-Wolf

intermediate temperature and moisture are covered with woodlands, grasslands, chaparral, and coastal scrub.

The effects of other important determinants of vegetation, such as soil fertility and depth, are influenced by topography and geology. These patterns are more easily seen at a finer scale than can be presented on the map at right. (See account entitled "Mojave Desert Vegetation" for a detailed map of vegetation types for a portion of the state.) Thus, within a general area climatically suitable for woodlands, we may see chaparral on shallower, steeper, and rockier soils; grasslands on deeper and less steep clay-rich soils; and woodlands on intermediate soils of gentle and moderate slope. The substrate on which vegetation grows may affect the species composition of certain broad types of vegetation. For example, vegetation on soils derived from serpentine, our state rock, may often be chaparral, but will be composed of very different species and be less dense than adjacent chaparral on soils derived from non-serpentine rock.

Coast redwood (*Sequoia sempervirens*) forest, Klamath/North Coast Region
Photo © Marc Hoshovsky

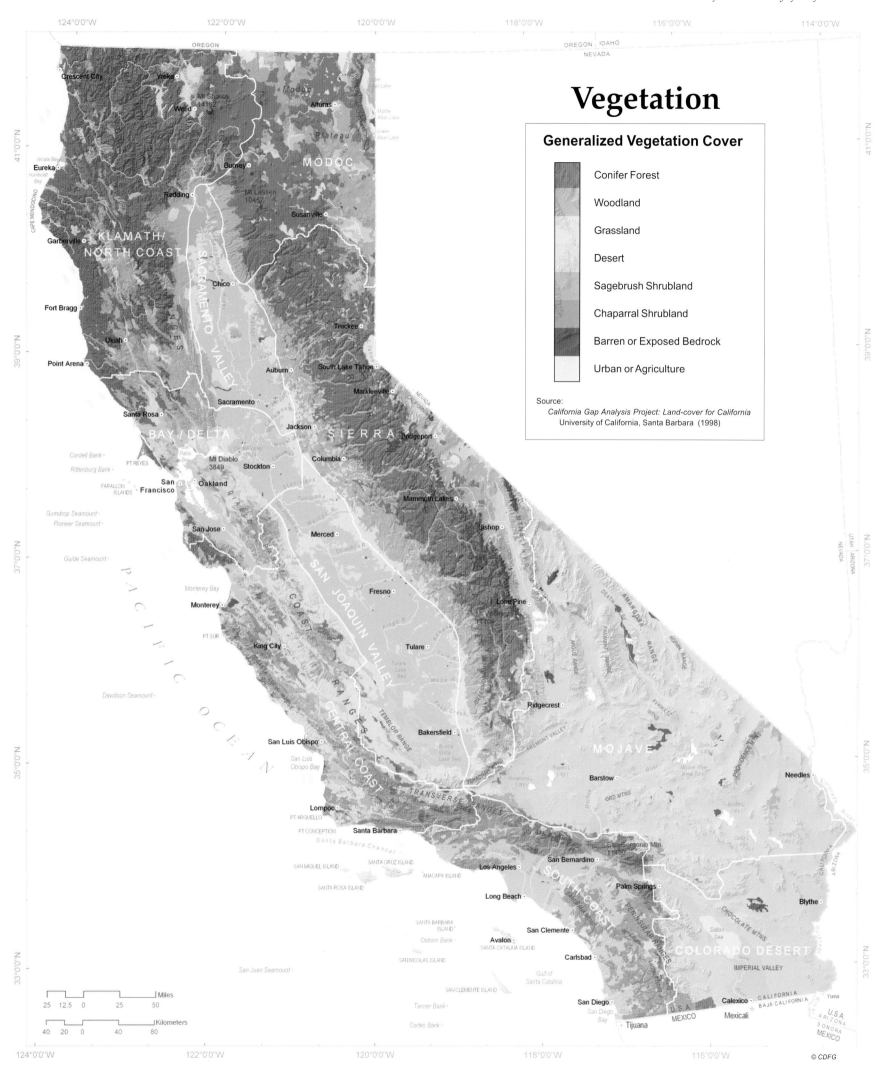

Vegetation

Generalized Vegetation Cover

Conifer Forest

Woodland

Grassland

Desert

Sagebrush Shrubland

Chaparral Shrubland

Barren or Exposed Bedrock

Urban or Agriculture

Source:
California Gap Analysis Project: Land-cover for California
University of California, Santa Barbara (1998)

© CDFG

Measures of Biodiversity

Richness, Rarity, and Endemism in California

Phrynosoma coronatum
COAST HORNED LIZARD

Areas of high richness, rarity, and endemism are found in every region of California. Even within a taxonomic group, such as plants or mammals, one region may support the highest total richness of species because of its climate and resulting vegetation. Another may support the highest concentrations of special status taxa or endemics because of its rare local geology or geographic isolation. Each region is unique in its contribution to the biodiversity of California.

Vegetation Types

By Todd Keeler-Wolf

The patterns across the land that all of us see, such as forests, woodlands, meadows, chaparral, and grasslands, may be described as different vegetation types. Vegetation types are similar in definition to ecosystems. However, they are defined primarily by their species rather than their non-living components,

Bristlecone pine (*Pinus longaeva*) alliance, Sierra Region
Photo © N.H. (Dan) Cheatham

such as soil, geology, climate, or topography. This implies that the reason we are interested in vegetation types has more to do with their biological uniqueness than with their other characteristics.

Sitka spruce (*Picea sitchensis*) forest alliance,
Klamath/North Coast Region
DFG photo: Todd Keeler-Wolf

Sampling in Douglas-fir (*Pseudotsuga menziesii*) forest alliance, Bay/Delta Region
DFG photo: Todd Keeler-Wolf

Allscale (*Atriplex polycarpa*)
alliance, Mojave Region
DFG photo: Todd Keeler-Wolf

One-sided bluegrass (*Poa secunda*) alliance with California poppy (*Eschscholzia californica*), Mojave Region
DFG photo: Todd Keeler-Wolf

California boasts a wealth of vegetation types, surpassing most other states. A recent assessment suggests that California may have over 2,000 distinct types of plant associations. This is almost half of the currently identified number of plant associations in the entire United States. Yet, the naming of vegetation types has only become systematic relatively recently. There are many more types to be identified. Currently, California has about 1,300 types defined (CDFG 2003a).

Vegetation types can be mapped and defined, making them a useful tool for ecological conservation and management. Ensuring the conservation of some of each of these types goes a long way toward maintaining the long term viability of any natural ecosystem.

How Vegetation Types are Classified in California

Vegetation types can be organized hierarchically from coarse to fine using concepts such as forest, woodland, shrubland, and grassland at the coarser levels and specific types of forest, woodland, shrubland, and grassland—each defined by characteristic species of plants—at the finer levels.

Quantitative sampling allows the definition of these finer levels. A plant alliance is generally based upon the dominant plant species in the uppermost or dominant layer of vegetation. A plant association is defined by the most characteristic species associated with a plant alliance. Many plant associations may be nested within a single plant alliance just like many species may be nested within a single genus.

Each defined vegetation type is ratified by a national panel of ecologists in much the same way as a new species is named and made valid. California's classification scheme for vegetation fits with the national vegetation classification scheme, as described in Grossman et al. (1998).

Todd Keeler-Wolf

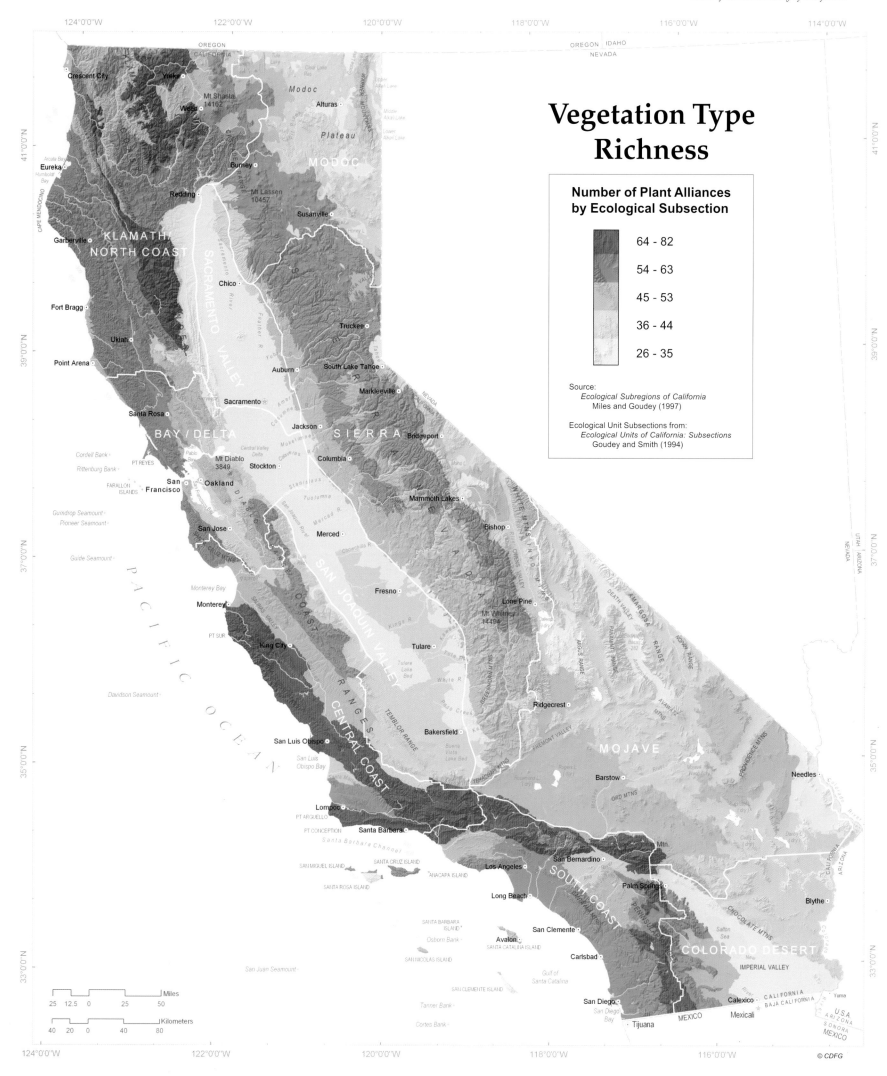

Vegetation Type Richness

**Number of Plant Alliances
by Ecological Subsection**

64 - 82

54 - 63

45 - 53

36 - 44

26 - 35

Source:
Ecological Subregions of California
Miles and Goudey (1997)

Ecological Unit Subsections from:
Ecological Units of California: Subsections
Goudey and Smith (1994)

© CDFG

Plants

By Roxanne Bittman

California contains some of the highest plant diversity in the world. It leads the nation in numbers of native plants. The latest figures indicate California has 6,272 plant taxa, including species and subspecies. Its 5,047 species (Jepson Flora Project 2002) represent 32 percent of the total number of plant species in the United States and nearly 25 percent of all the plant taxa found in North America north of the Mexican border. California also has an enormous number of endemic plants. Its 2,153 endemic taxa represent over one third of its native plants.

Chaparral clusterlily (*Brodiaea jolonensis*)
Photo: John Game

Dune primrose (*Oenothera deltoides*) and desert sand verbena (*Abronia villosa*)
Photo © Rodney Temples

Reasons for this plant diversity stem from the unique combination of Mediterranean climate and topographic, geologic, and soils diversity. In addition, many taxa from the Tertiary Period, such as the giant sequoia (*Sequoiadendron giganteum*), have survived here due to our mild climate. Finally, over geological time, outbursts of speciation have occurred among some groups of plants, such as the wildflowers.

The map of California plant richness comes from data provided by the Jepson Flora Project in 2002. The dataset was created by assigning each plant in *The Jepson Manual: Higher Plants of California* (Hickman 1993) to a geographic subregion as defined in the manual. The map displays the total number of California native plant taxa present in each Jepson geographic subregion. As with any simplified map, a number of assumptions have been made, and as the data are refined, a different picture may emerge. However, the general patterns follow the basic driving ecological factors known to most strongly influence plant distribution and diversity.

Five-spot (*Nemophila maculata*)
Photo © Barbara J. Nelson

Vegetation and plant species closely follow shifts in moisture and temperature as produced by topography and accompanying climate. The topographic and moisture gradients in the Sierra Nevada are the most extreme in the state, followed by those in the Klamath Mountains and in the San Bernardino Mountains. Thus, the map at right shows the richest plant diversity in the high Sierra and Klamath areas, with the next richest areas being the outer North Coast ranges, the Cascades, and the San Bernardino Mountains. Lowest in plant richness are the desert and Central Valley areas.

Compare this map and the special status plant map that follows. Rare plant richness may more closely follow geologic variation than does overall plant richness, and thus the Klamath, desert mountain ranges, and several coastal areas are rare plant hotspots. Also, the high level of rarity in the Bay/Delta and South Coast regions may reflect the greater level of habitat destruction in those regions than in the Sierra, where total plant richness is high.

Crinkled onion
(*Allium crispum*)
Photo: John Game

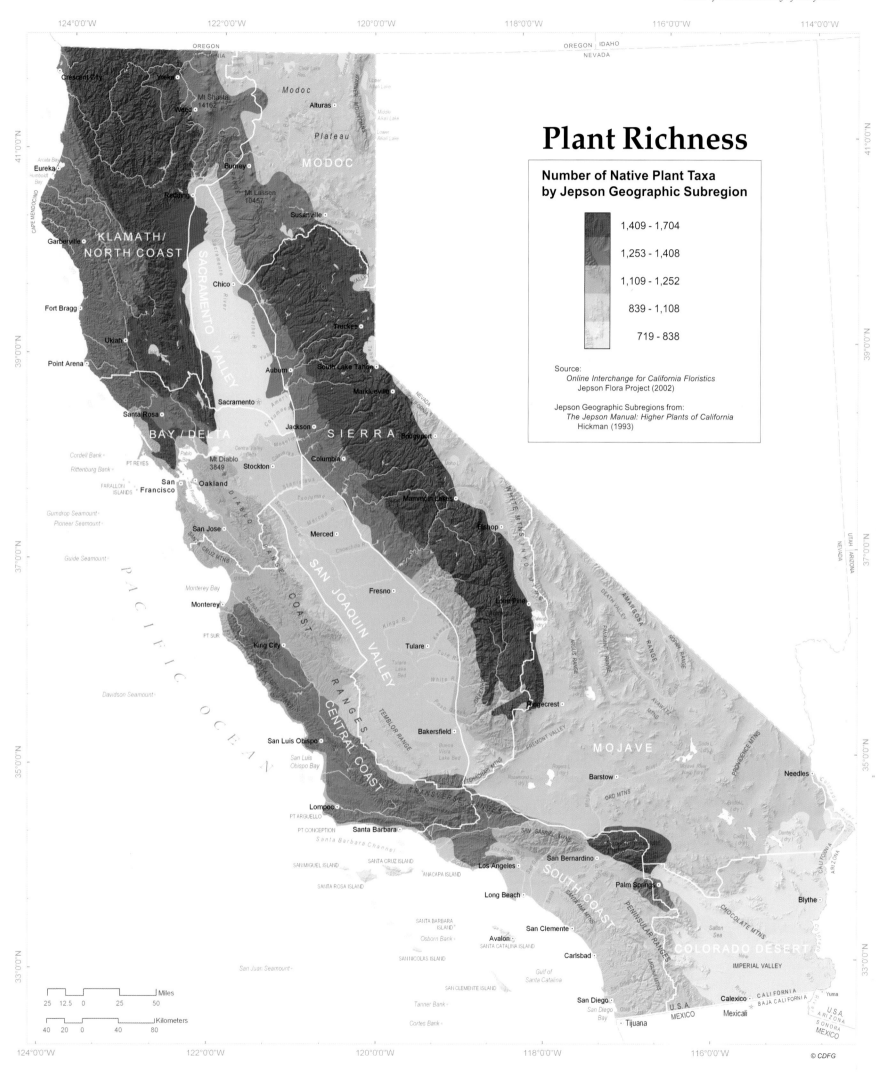

Plant Richness

Number of Native Plant Taxa by Jepson Geographic Subregion

1,409 - 1,704

1,253 - 1,408

1,109 - 1,252

839 - 1,108

719 - 838

Source:
Online Interchange for California Floristics
Jepson Flora Project (2002)

Jepson Geographic Subregions from:
The Jepson Manual: Higher Plants of California
Hickman (1993)

© CDFG

Special Status Plants

By Roxanne Bittman

With 2,089 special status plant taxa, California has more special status plants than any other state in the nation. This figure represents about 30 percent of all the native plants in the state. Hawaii has the next highest number, with 658 special status plant taxa.

The list for California includes both plants that are naturally low in numbers due to restricted habitats, and plants that have become this way due to human activities. California's rich flora has both high levels of innate rarity and some of the most intense development pressure anywhere in the nation.

Agriculture has converted nearly all of the land in the Central Valley, home for many special status vernal pool plants. Residential development has been primarily concentrated on the coast and is moving inland and into the Sierra foothills, threatening hundreds of species. Invasive, introduced plants have further displaced the native flora and are a serious threat to many plant populations. (See the "Pressures on Biodiversity" section later in this book.)

California's varied geology and soils help answer the question as to why California is so rich in special status plant species. The table at right illustrates the numbers of special status plants found on different substrates, with serpentine-derived soils taking the lead in special status plant diversity in California. The properties of serpentine soil create a very harsh environment for plants. (See account entitled "Geology and Soils.") Only a select group has evolved to withstand its conditions. Also, invasive, introduced plants tend to do very poorly on serpentine, so there is little competition from these species. Serpentine outcrops tend to act like "islands" for native plants since the

outcrops are often discontinuous and separated by non-serpentine expanses. Plants have evolved into many unique forms on the individual outcrops due to this combination of special environmental factors and isolation. Granitics, clays, carbonates, and volcanics also provide habitat for many special status plants.

Unlike the rarity hotspots for groups such as reptiles (page 31), rare plant hotspots are spread fairly evenly throughout the state. In addition, because there are simply more special status plants than animals, the number of species reflected in the "low" legend category for rare plants is comparable to the "high" legend category for amphibians, birds, fish, reptiles, mammals, and invertebrates. While rarity hotspots exist throughout the state, particularly rich areas for rare plant diversity occur in the greater San Francisco Bay area and western San Diego County. The large number of rare plants in these two areas reflects both ecological reality as well as the effects of human activity on the environment.

Cirsium loncholepis

L A   G R A C I O S A
T H I S T L E

Substrate Preferences of Special Status Plants
After CNPS (1997), updated based on CNPS (2001)

Substrate	Number of Special Status Plant Taxa
Serpentine	298
Granite	126
Clay	113
Carbonate	111
Volcanic	99
Alkaline	82
Gabbro	20
Sandstone	19
Shale	10
Gypsum	1

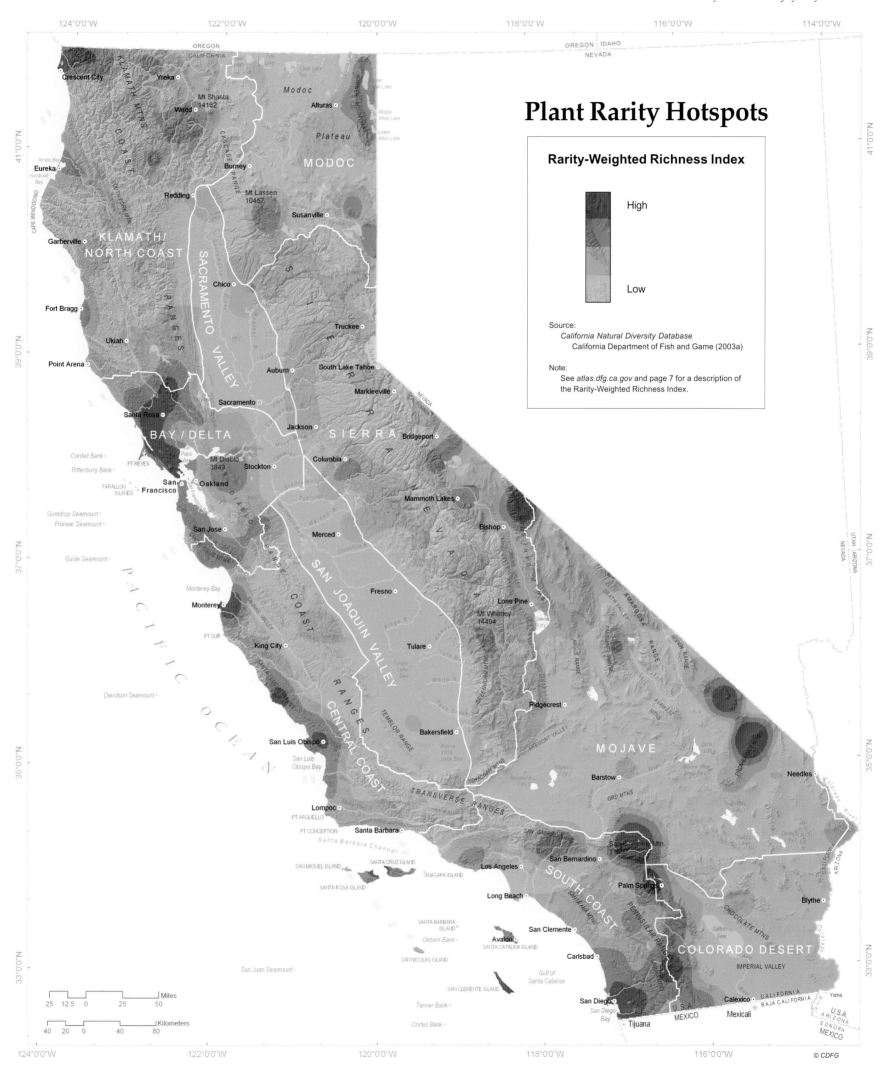

Plant Rarity Hotspots

Rarity-Weighted Richness Index

High

Low

Source:
California Natural Diversity Database
California Department of Fish and Game (2003a)

Note:
See *atlas.dfg.ca.gov* and page 7 for a description of the Rarity-Weighted Richness Index.

© CDFG

Amphibians

By Kathy Hill

California is home to 51 native species of amphibians (CDFG and CIWTG 2002). The amphibians include frogs, toads, and salamanders.

California tiger salamander (*Ambystoma tigrinum californiense*)
Photo: Gerald and Buff Corsi, California Academy of Sciences

Frogs and toads have a complex life cycle, which includes two fully aquatic stages and a terrestrial or partially aquatic stage. The fully aquatic stages are the egg and the tadpole (or pollywog) stages. Tadpoles obtain their oxygen and food from the water, and depend on cryptic coloration or toxic skin secretions to avoid predators. Their food usually consists of algae, which grows on rocks or other structures in their aquatic environment, but some tadpoles are also carnivorous.

After several weeks or months, a tadpole undergoes a transformation by absorbing its tail, growing legs, and changing mouthparts. The new body form allows it to take advantage of terrestrial food resources, obtain oxygen from the air, and move upland to another area. This transformation is adaptive, especially in seasonal wetlands, which dry up in the summer or fall.

Many frogs and toads use sounds to attract mates and to defend territories. The loud chirping of male Pacific chorus frogs (*Pseudacris regilla*) is a well-known springtime evening sound.
Photo © Rodney Temples

Western spadefoot toad (*Spea hammondii*)
Photo © Bill Basom

Amphibians favor wet places, and species diversity is highest in those parts of California where precipitation is high, as in the Klamath/North Coast Region. Amphibians have moist, absorbent skin. Some frogs and salamanders that live in very moist areas do not have lungs; they breathe through their skin. However, amphibians range throughout California, including the drier grasslands and deserts. Those few amphibians that live in the deserts of California still need moisture. Some live near permanent desert springs, like the red-spotted toad (*Bufo punctatus*), but the spadefoot toads are able to live in places that dry up completely each year. They use their "spade" feet to dig into the drying mud and then their skin secretes a layer of mucous that keeps their bodies moist throughout the dry months.

Klamath/North Coast Region

The Klamath/North Coast Region in California's northwestern corner is famous for its rocky coastline, salmon fishing, and lush mountain forests of spectacular ancient coast redwood (*Sequoia sempervirens*) and Douglas-fir (*Pseudotsuga menziesii*). It has the wettest climate in the state, with rainfall distribution varying widely from an average annual 38 inches at Fort Bragg to 120 or more inches east of Crescent City. The coastal climate is cool, moist, and often foggy, with rainy winters at lower elevations and snow in the higher mountains. Inland, the climate is drier, with low rainfall in the winter and hot, dry summers. Dominant plants include coast redwood, Douglas-fir, ponderosa pine (*Pinus ponderosa*), tanoak (*Lithocarpus densiflorus*), incense cedar (*Calocedrus decurrens*), and chaparral species.

Marc Hoshovsky

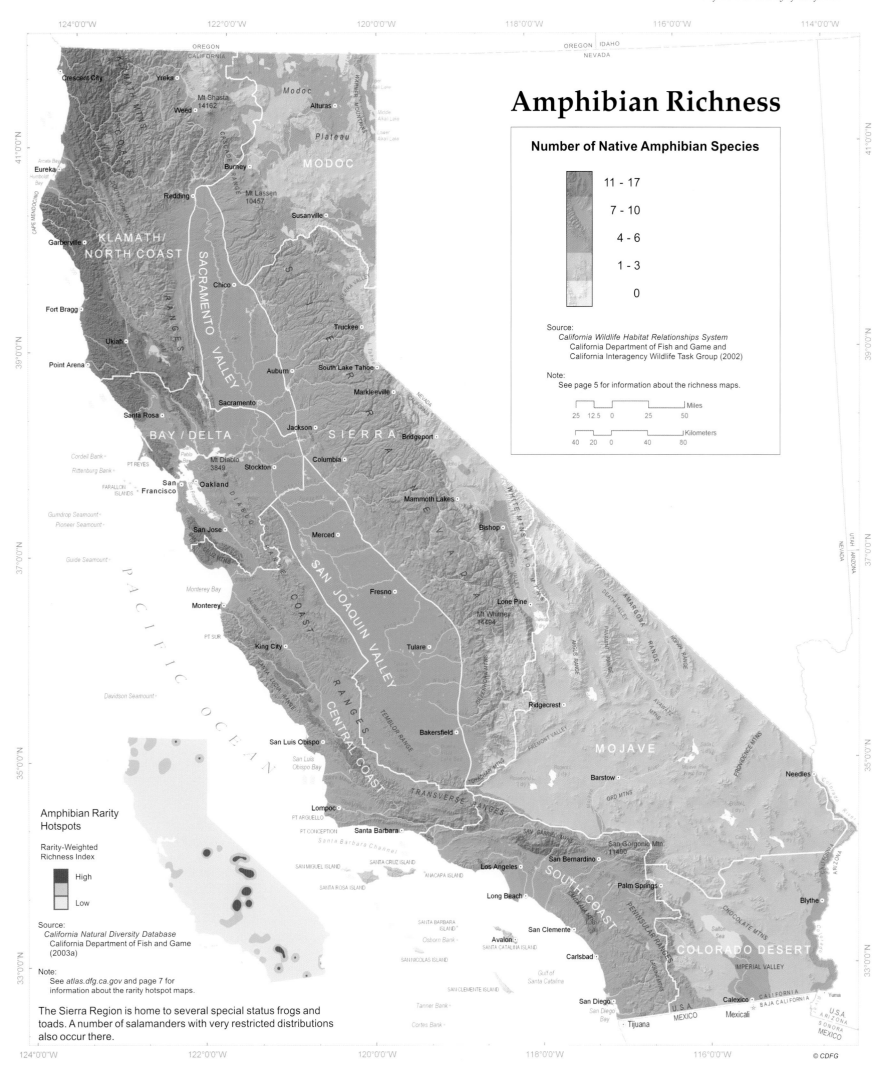

Amphibian Richness

Number of Native Amphibian Species

11 - 17

7 - 10

4 - 6

1 - 3

0

Source:
California Wildlife Habitat Relationships System
California Department of Fish and Game and
California Interagency Wildlife Task Group (2002)

Note:
See page 5 for information about the richness maps.

Miles
25 12.5 0 25 50

Kilometers
40 20 0 40 80

Amphibian Rarity Hotspots

Rarity-Weighted
Richness Index

High

Low

Source:
California Natural Diversity Database
California Department of Fish and Game
(2003a)

Note:
See atlas.dfg.ca.gov and page 7 for
information about the rarity hotspot maps.

The Sierra Region is home to several special status frogs and toads. A number of salamanders with very restricted distributions also occur there.

© CDFG

Reptiles

By Kathy Hill

Baja California collared lizard
(*Crotaphytus vestigium*)
Photo © Sherburn R. Sanborn

There are 84 native species of reptiles in California, including lizards, snakes, and turtles (CDFG and CIWTG 2002). Reptiles are considered cold-blooded because their body temperature is determined by their surrounding environment. To warm up in the morning, reptiles will bask in the sun on dark colored surfaces, which absorb heat readily. This is why snakes and lizards are often seen on roads; the dark asphalt helps them warm up quickly.

Although there are reptiles in nearly all of California, most species are found in the desert areas because reptiles are well adapted to that extreme environment. Despite being called cold-blooded, many reptiles have optimum body temperatures much warmer than normal human temperature. For instance, the desert iguana (*Dipsosaurus dorsalis*) of the Mojave and Colorado deserts can be seen running around on the hottest summer days. Reptiles also have scale-covered skin, which keeps them from losing moisture, and thus protects them from a hot, dry environment.

Desert iguana (*Dipsosaurus dorsalis*)
Photo © Peter L. Knapp

California has 45 taxa of native snakes. Certain places, like the Sierra Nevada foothills, are high in snake species diversity. The trees, rock outcrops, and caves of the foothills provide cover in a variety of habitats. The foothills also provide protection from winter flooding. In California's natural hydrology, much of the valley floor was flooded during the winter and spring months and provided habitat for aquatic reptiles such as garter snakes (*Thamnophis* spp.) and western pond turtles (*Clemmys marmorata*). However, these Central Valley reptiles also require non-flooding habitats above the flood plain, such as hills, levees, and rock outcrops, for winter hibernation.

Of all the snakes in California, only the rattlesnakes (*Crotalus* spp.) can be dangerous to humans. Rattlesnakes use their venom to subdue prey, which are mainly rodents. They also use venom to defend themselves if they are threatened.
Photo © David Welling

Mojave and Colorado Desert Regions

The Mojave and Colorado deserts together range up to 4,000 feet in elevation and cover most of the southeastern part of the state. These regions are the home of three national parks and monuments—Death Valley, East Mojave, and Joshua Tree—as well as Anza-Borrego Desert State Park, the largest state park in the country. The Mojave Desert is located north of the Colorado Desert, at elevations above 1,000 feet. Creosote scrub dominates most of the Mojave, with Joshua tree (*Yucca brevifolia*) and a greater variety of shrubs at higher elevations. The Colorado Desert, named for its proximity to the lower Colorado River, is actually part of the more extensive Sonoran Desert, which extends east to Arizona and south to Mexico. Vegetation includes cactus scrub, desert wash woodlands, palm oases, saltbush scrub, and alkali sink scrub.

Marc Hoshovsky

Desert tortoise (*Gopherus agassizii*)
Photo © Karen Wyatt

Mojave fringe-toed lizard (*Uma scoparia*)
DFG photo: Tom King

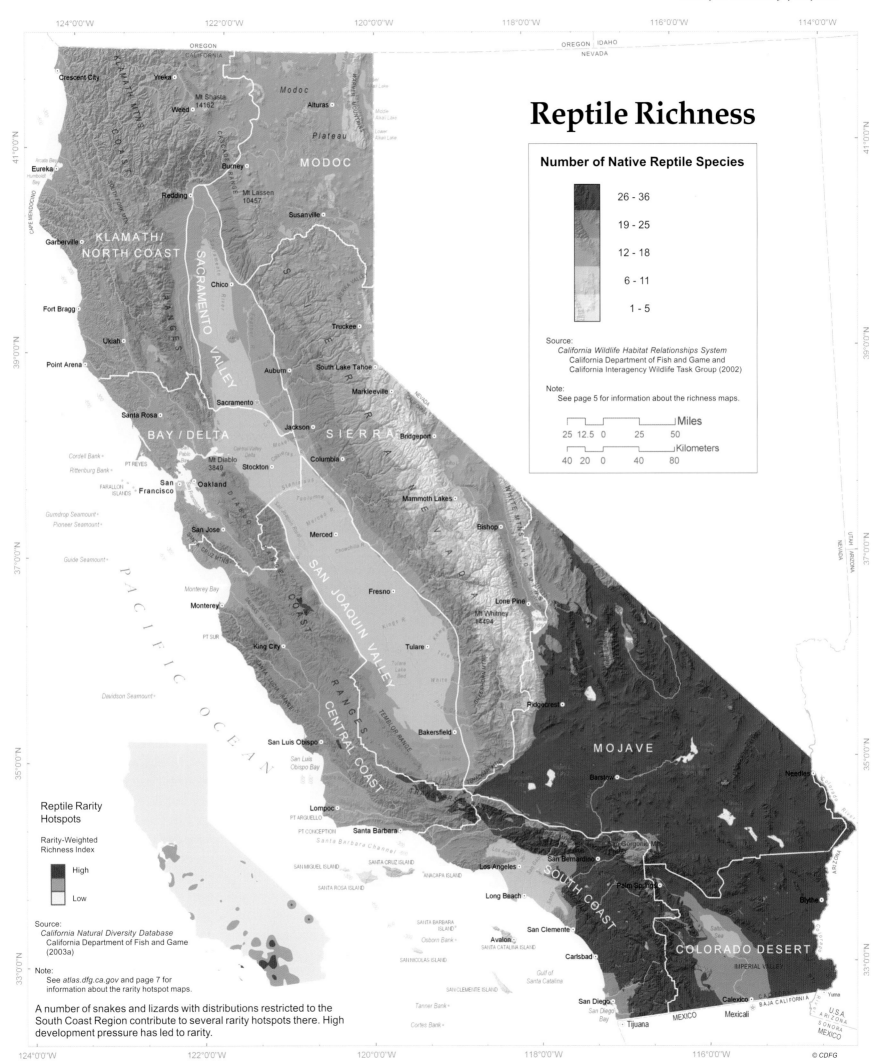

Reptile Richness

Number of Native Reptile Species

26 - 36

19 - 25

12 - 18

6 - 11

1 - 5

Source:
California Wildlife Habitat Relationships System
California Department of Fish and Game and
California Interagency Wildlife Task Group (2002)

Note:
See page 5 for information about the richness maps.

Miles
25 12.5 0   25   50

Kilometers
40   20   0   40   80

Reptile Rarity Hotspots

Rarity-Weighted
Richness Index

High

Low

Source:
California Natural Diversity Database
California Department of Fish and Game
(2003a)

Note:
See *atlas.dfg.ca.gov* and page 7 for
information about the rarity hotspot maps.

A number of snakes and lizards with distributions restricted to the
South Coast Region contribute to several rarity hotspots there. High
development pressure has led to rarity.

© CDFG

Birds

By Barrett Garrison

Of all the wild animals inhabiting California, birds are some of the most active and visible. Birds are found everywhere, from the top of Mount Whitney to the bottom of Death Valley, and from the middle of our most populated cities to the most remote and uninhabited wild places. Birds use every available habitat here, including the Pacific Ocean, our lakes and rivers, forests and woodlands, grasslands, and deserts.

A total of 602 native species have been known to occur in California at some point during their life cycle (CDFG and CIWTG 2002). Since records have been kept, an astounding 325 species have bred here at one time or another. California has two species found nowhere else in the world—Island Scrub-Jay (*Aphelocoma insularis*) and Yellow-billed Magpie (*Pica nuttalli*). And, seven species are virtually confined to California—Ashy Storm-Petrel (*Oceanodroma homochroa*), Nuttall's Woodpecker (*Picoides nuttallii*), Oak Titmouse (*Baeolophus inornatus*), Wrentit (*Chamaea fasciata*), California Thrasher (*Toxostoma redivivum*), Lawrence's Goldfinch (*Carduelis lawrencei*), and Tricolored Blackbird (*Agelaius tricolor*).

Allen's Hummingbird (*Selasphorus sasin*)
Photo © Hugh P. Smith, Jr.

Until recently released into Arizona's Grand Canyon, California Condor (*Gymnogyps californianus*) in the last century was confined in range to this state. In addition, there are numerous subspecies found only in California. California's large size, varied topography, mild climate, and habitat diversity are largely responsible for the state's uniquely rich bird life.

Wrentit (*Chamaea fasciata*)
Photo © James Gallagher

Yellow-billed Magpies (*Pica nuttalli*)
Photo © Douglas Herr

California's birds are generally categorized by whether they migrate or not. About one quarter of California's native bird species are known as residents because they remain here all year and do not migrate. Between one third and one half of its birds are known as migrants. These include species that regularly migrate to California to breed in the summer, like Allen's Hummingbird (*Selasphorus sasin*), species that spend the winter in California, and species that only pass through during spring or fall migrations. Finally, about one third are known as vagrants. They do not occur here regularly because their breeding or wintering ranges or migratory routes are normally outside of California.

Summer

Summer bird species richness includes residents and summer migrants. Most of these migrants breed in California. The greatest number of breeding species occurs in the woody vegetation of the coastal regions, foothills, and mountains and valleys of northeastern California. Fewer species breed in the arid desert regions, high elevation mountain zones, and the Central Valley. In areas richest in breeding species, a large proportion of the species are migrants. However, even areas that are low in breeding species richness are important because they support a high proportion of residents with restricted ranges. For example, Gambel's Quail (*Callipepla gambelii*), Cactus Wren (*Campylorhynchus brunneicapillus*), Verdin (*Auriparus flaviceps*), and Le Conte's Thrasher (*Toxostoma lecontei*) occur primarily in California's desert regions. These regions do not support a large number of bird species, as can be seen on the following maps.

(continued)

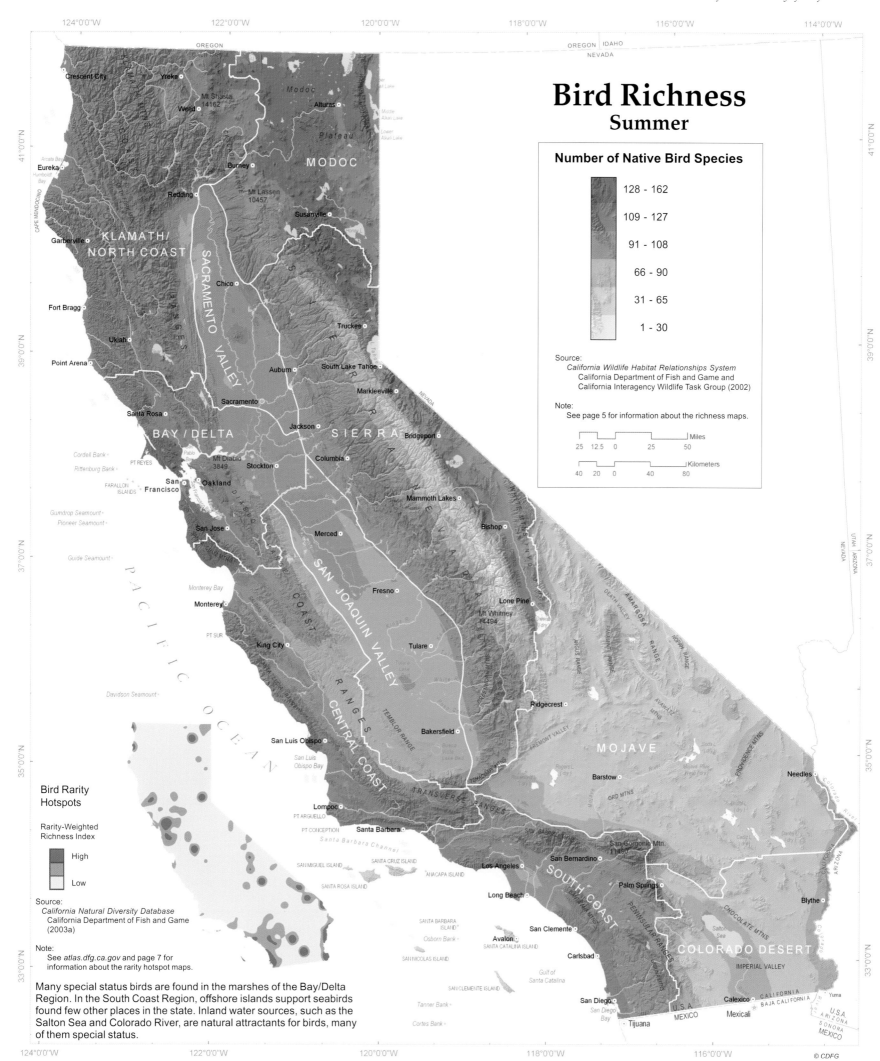

Bird Richness
Summer

Number of Native Bird Species

	128 - 162
	109 - 127
	91 - 108
	66 - 90
	31 - 65
	1 - 30

Source:
California Wildlife Habitat Relationships System
California Department of Fish and Game and
California Interagency Wildlife Task Group (2002)

Note:
See page 5 for information about the richness maps.

Miles
25 12.5 0   25   50

Kilometers
40 20 0   40   80

Bird Rarity Hotspots

Rarity-Weighted
Richness Index

High

Low

Source:
California Natural Diversity Database
California Department of Fish and Game
(2003a)

Note:
See atlas.dfg.ca.gov and page 7 for
information about the rarity hotspot maps.

Many special status birds are found in the marshes of the Bay/Delta
Region. In the South Coast Region, offshore islands support seabirds
found few other places in the state. Inland water sources, such as the
Salton Sea and Colorado River, are natural attractants for birds, many
of them special status.

© CDFG

Birds

(continued from page 32)

Winter

Winter bird species richness includes residents and winter migrants. The pattern for wintering species is dramatically different from that of summer breeding species. Winter species richness is highest in the coastal regions, the Central Valley, the foothills and mountains of Southern California, along the Colorado River, and around the Salton Sea. Species richness during winter is lowest in the Sierra Nevada, deserts, and mountains and mountain valleys of Northern California.

Snow Geese (*Chen caerulescens*)
Photo © Frank Kratofil

Canada Geese (*Branta canadensis*) at Tule Lake National Wildlife Refuge, Modoc Region
Photo © Susan Van Der Wal

The seasonal reduction in species from these regions is due to extreme winter weather conditions that drive migrants into areas with warmer and milder climates. The large number of wintering species along the coast includes ducks, geese, and shorebirds that migrate to California, as well as marine species such as loons and grebes, and landbirds that reside in the wooded hills and towns along the coast.

Central Coast and South Coast Regions

The Central Coast Region extends from just north of Santa Cruz to just south of Santa Barbara. It consists mostly of coastal mountains with small inland valleys. The region has a mild, seasonally moist, and sometimes foggy climate. Vegetation includes oak woodlands, chaparral, grasslands, and, in the northern part of the region, patches of coast redwood (*Sequoia sempervirens*) forest.

The South Coast Region extends from Ventura County to the Mexican border and east to the edge of the Mojave and Colorado deserts. Hot, dry summers that create conditions for wildfires are followed by wet winters with storms that can trigger mudslides where fire has denuded slopes. This is the most densely populated region of the state. Vegetation includes coastal scrub, chaparral, grasslands, live oak woodlands, and riparian forests.

Marc Hoshovsky

Marbled Godwits (*Limosa fedoa*)
Photo © Ed Ely

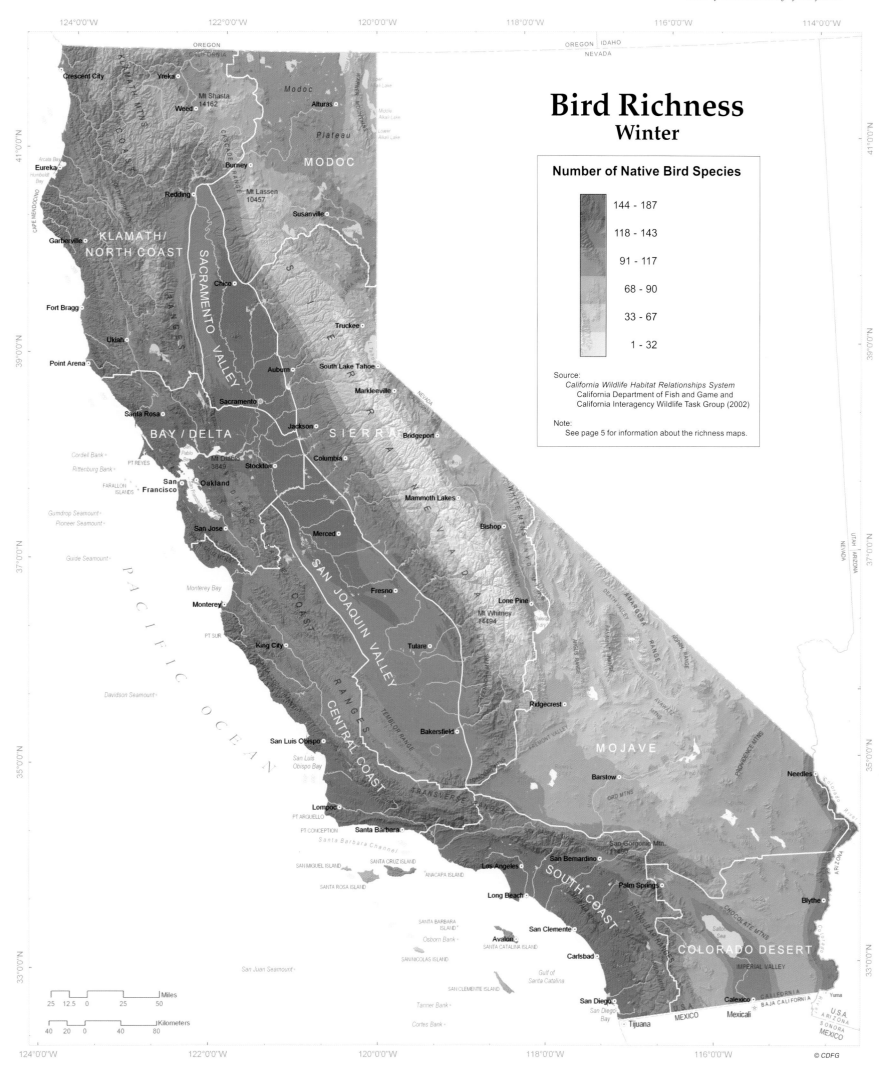

Bird Richness
Winter

Number of Native Bird Species

144 - 187

118 - 143

91 - 117

68 - 90

33 - 67

1 - 32

Source:
California Wildlife Habitat Relationships System
California Department of Fish and Game and
California Interagency Wildlife Task Group (2002)

Note:
See page 5 for information about the richness maps.

Waterfowl

By Melanie Weaver

California hosts 40 different species and subspecies of waterfowl, which include ducks, geese, and swans. About 27 species are found in the Sacramento Valley and San Joaquin Valley regions in winter. Included in these winter visitors are more than 90 percent of the Tule Greater White-fronted Goose (*Anser albifrons gambelli*) and Aleutian Canada Goose (*Branta canadensis leucopareia*) populations, and up to 65 percent of the continent's Northern Pintail (*Anas acuta*).

Northern Pintail (*Anas acuta*)
Photo © Brian O'Neill

Most waterfowl are migratory birds. The majority of them breed in Canada and Alaska and fly south for the winter to California and Mexico. Waterfowl and other migratory birds endure the risks of migration to enhance their survival. The breeding areas in the north typically freeze over in winter making food unattainable, but many sources of food become available during winter elsewhere on the continent. Some species, like Mallard (*Anas platyrhynchos*), Gadwall (*Anas strepera*), Cinnamon Teal (*Anas cyanoptera*), and Canada Goose (*Branta canadensis*), include populations that remain year round in California.

Gadwall (*Anas strepera*)
Photo © John C. Muegge

The migration routes that waterfowl use between breeding and winter areas are aggregated geographically into flyways. North America has four flyways: Pacific, Central, Mississippi, and Atlantic. California provides vital winter habitat for about 60 percent of the waterfowl population in the Pacific Flyway. This is estimated to be between 4 and 6 million birds per year. In the winter, the greatest concentration of waterfowl is found in the Central Valley. Its 16,000 square miles include 12,000 square miles of some of the world's most productive agricultural lands. Historically, there were an estimated 4 million acres of seasonal wetlands. Only about 170,000 acres remain, the majority of which are privately owned.

Mallard (*Anas platyrhynchos*)
Photo © Russ Kerr

Waterfowl occur in the Sacramento Valley and San Joaquin Valley regions because some agricultural lands and the remaining wetlands provide the nutrition and other requirements necessary for survival. Waterfowl feed largely upon agricultural grain left over after harvest, as well as wild seeds, grasses, tubers, and invertebrates. These foods ensure survival over winter and provide reserves of fat necessary to sustain long flights back to the northern breeding grounds.

Sacramento Valley and San Joaquin Valley Regions

The Sacramento and San Joaquin valleys separate the Sierra Nevada from the Coast Ranges. Along with the eastern portion of the Bay/Delta Region, these areas are collectively known as the Central Valley. The Sacramento Valley and San Joaquin Valley regions have hot, dry summers followed by winters with frequent rainstorms (except during occasional droughts). Fog blankets the valley during the winter season, keeping temperatures low. However, snowfall is unusual because daytime temperatures typically remain above freezing. Most of the water that falls in the state drains down the Central Valley's two major rivers, the Sacramento and the San Joaquin, and flows out through the Sacramento-San Joaquin Delta. Although now dominated by agriculture, the valley still harbors important oak woodlands, riparian forests, wetlands, and grasslands.

Marc Hoshovsky

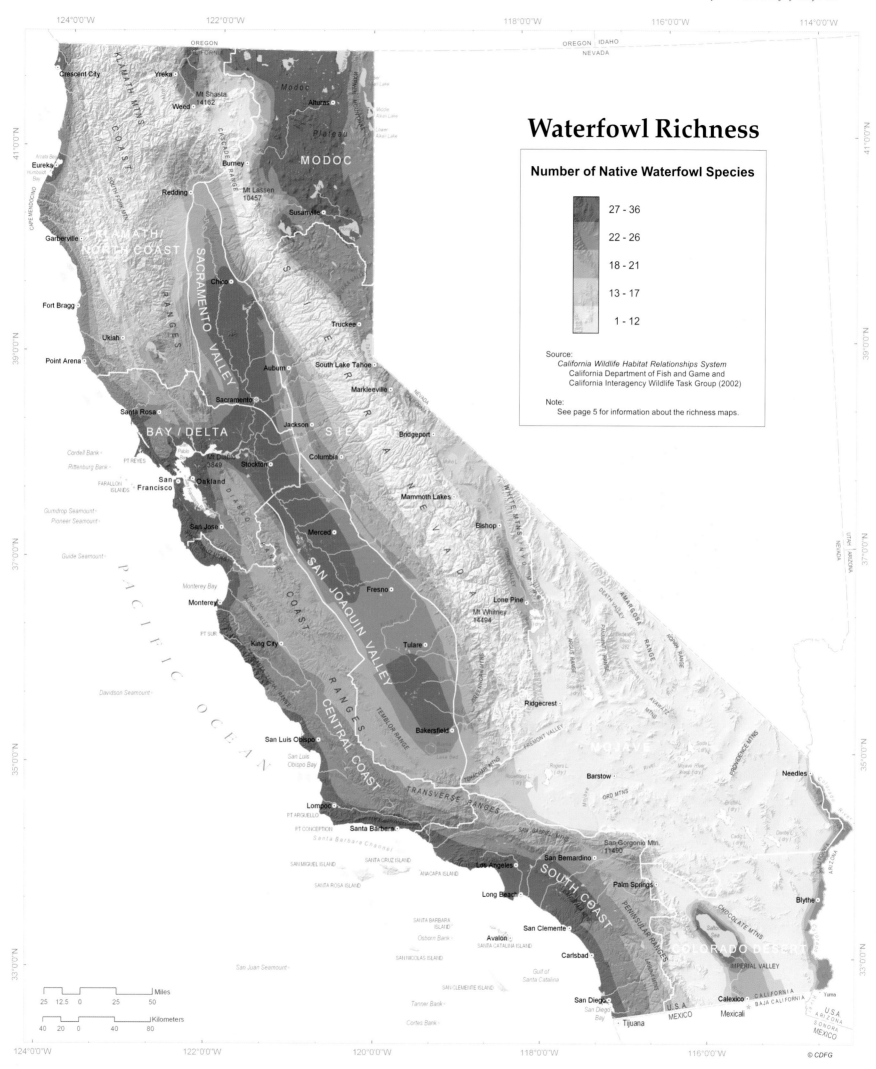

Waterfowl Richness

Number of Native Waterfowl Species

27 - 36

22 - 26

18 - 21

13 - 17

1 - 12

Source:
California Wildlife Habitat Relationships System
California Department of Fish and Game and
California Interagency Wildlife Task Group (2002)

Note:
See page 5 for information about the richness maps.

© CDFG

Mammals

By Monica Parisi

So often when the term "wild animal" is used, it is a mammal which immediately comes to mind. Mammals are warm-blooded animals, usually covered with fur or hair, that nurse their young through mammary glands. This class of vertebrates includes everything from shrews to bats to foxes to whales. A significant 197 native mammal species occur in California (CDFG and CIWTG 2002).

Large mammals such as mule deer (*Odocoileus hemionus*) and mountain lion *(Puma concolor)* are the best known. However, the majority of mammal species in California are relatively small. The greatest species richness is found in the squirrel and chipmunk family and in the woodrat and vole family. Many of the species in these families rely on forested habitats, so it is not surprising that species richness is high where forest vegetation is abundant. This is true in the Klamath/North Coast, Modoc, and Sierra regions. Pocket mice and kangaroo rats, all well adapted to arid climates, account for much of the species richness on the eastern side of the Modoc and Sierra regions and in the Colorado Desert. Kangaroo rats even have specialized kidneys which excrete solid urine, allowing them to survive for long periods without drinking water.

The list of endemic mammal species includes the state-threatened island gray fox (*Urocyon littoralis*), found only on the Channel Islands.
Photo courtesy of National Park Service

Although California shares its high mammal species richness with several southwestern states, it has by far the highest mammal endemism of any state in the country. California has 17 endemic mammal species. Alaska follows with seven, and Oregon with three (Stein et al. 2000). Endemism is unusually high in the Sacramento and San Joaquin Valley regions. Three species and 22 subspecies of mammals endemic to the state occur in the Central Valley.

Big-eared kangaroo rat
(*Dipodomys venustus* ssp.
santaluciae), a subspecies of
narrow-faced kangaroo rat
Photo © Caitlin Bean

Geographic isolation is one factor that contributes to endemism, and the southwestern portion of the San Joaquin Valley provides an example. Several endemic mammal species or subspecies have evolved in the arid grassland and scrub habitats found there. Evidence suggests that between 4,000 and 8,000 years ago, dry climatic conditions allowed the extension of desert species from east of the Sierra Nevada into the San Joaquin Valley through various passes. When cooler and moister conditions returned, many populations became isolated from the Mojave Desert by bands of woodland and chaparral habitats (Bradford 1992).

Multi-agency recovery efforts for special status species include a plan for the San Joaquin Valley (Williams et al. 1997) that addresses several endemic mammals. The plan contains strategies for protecting lands on which these species already occur from incompatible uses and restoring habitat value to lands that can serve as movement corridors between isolated patches of habitat.

Mammal Species Endemic to California	
Mount Lyell shrew	*Sorex lyelli*
Alpine chipmunk	*Tamias alpinus*
Sonoma chipmunk	*Tamias sonomae*
Yellow-cheeked chipmunk	*Tamias ochrogenys*
San Joaquin antelope squirrel	*Ammospermophilus nelsoni*
Mohave ground squirrel	*Spermophilus mohavensis*
San Joaquin pocket mouse	*Perognathus inornatus*
White-eared pocket mouse	*Perognathus alticolus*
Narrow-faced kangaroo rat	*Dipodomys venustus*
Pacific kangaroo rat	*Dipodomys agilis*
Heerman's kangaroo rat	*Dipodomys heermanni*
Giant kangaroo rat	*Dipodomys ingens*
Stephen's kangaroo rat	*Dipodomys stephensi*
Fresno kangaroo rat	*Dipodomys nitratoides*
Salt-marsh harvest mouse	*Reithrodontomys raviventris*
California red tree vole	*Arborimus pomo*
Island gray fox	*Urocyon littoralis*

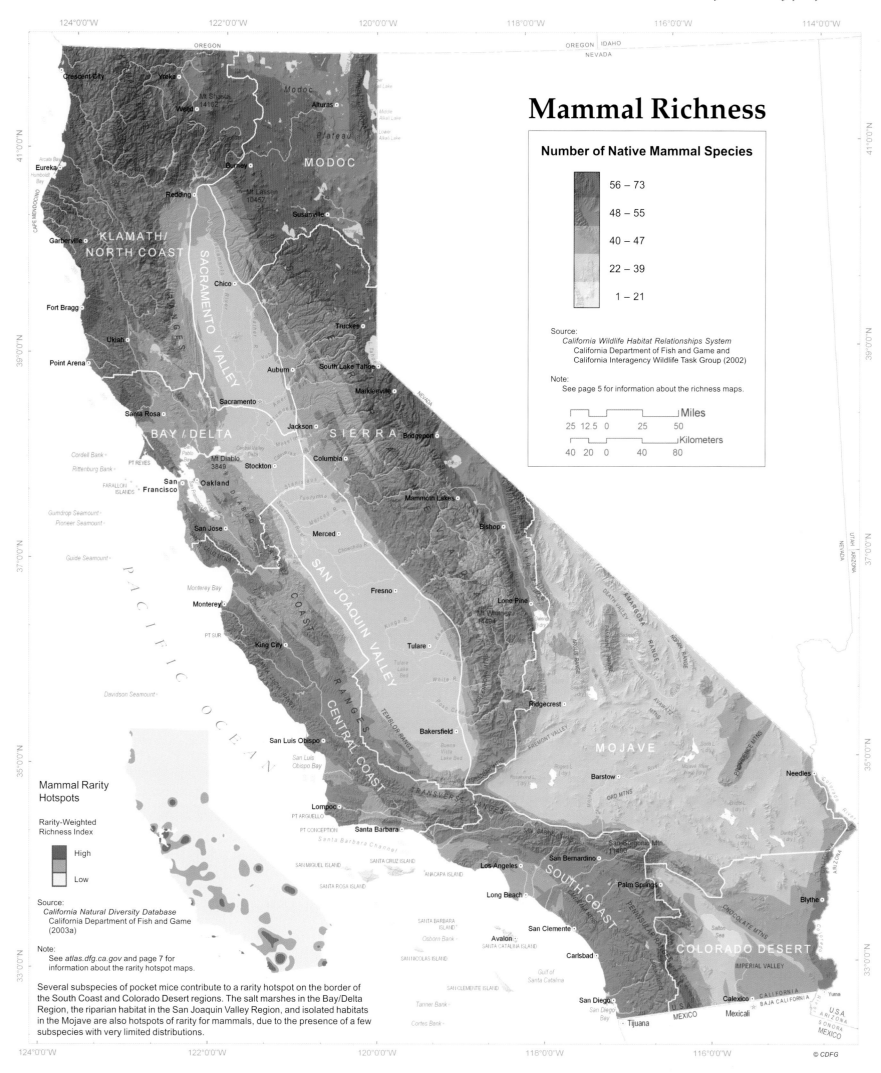

Mammal Richness

Number of Native Mammal Species

56 – 73
48 – 55
40 – 47
22 – 39
1 – 21

Source:
California Wildlife Habitat Relationships System
California Department of Fish and Game and
California Interagency Wildlife Task Group (2002)

Note:
See page 5 for information about the richness maps.

Miles
25 12.5 0   25   50

Kilometers
40 20 0   40   80

Mammal Rarity Hotspots

Rarity-Weighted
Richness Index

High

Low

Source:
California Natural Diversity Database
California Department of Fish and Game
(2003a)

Note:
See *atlas.dfg.ca.gov* and page 7 for
information about the rarity hotspot maps.

Several subspecies of pocket mice contribute to a rarity hotspot on the border of
the South Coast and Colorado Desert regions. The salt marshes in the Bay/Delta
Region, the riparian habitat in the San Joaquin Valley Region, and isolated habitats
in the Mojave are also hotspots of rarity for mammals, due to the presence of a few
subspecies with very limited distributions.

© CDFG

Selected Wide-Ranging Mammals

By Eric Loft

The most widely recognized animal species in California include the medium to large sized mammals that inhabit nearly all wild areas of the state. Most of these species also have large home ranges, and some may require thousands of acres of contiguous habitat for their populations to remain viable.

The reasons for needing extensive ranges may differ among species. For example, herds of mule deer (*Odocoileus hemionus*) and pronghorn (*Antilocapra americana*) cross up to 100 miles of habitat traveling between summer and winter ranges in northeastern California. Predators, such as mountain lion (*Puma concolor*) and fisher (*Martes pennanti*), are typically solitary and may cover thousands of acres as individuals in their search for food; thousands more acres are required to sustain entire populations.

The distributions of 24 wide-ranging, native mammal species were compiled for this atlas. They range from abundant, such as mule deer and coyote (*Canis latrans*), to common, such as black bear (*Ursus americanus*), to rarely seen, such as mountain beaver (*Aplodontia rufa*) and fisher. The wolverine (*Gulo gulo*) has not been confirmed to occur in the state for many years, although there are occasional reports of sightings.

Pronghorn (*Antilocapra americana*)
Photo © Karen McClymonds

The intent of selecting these species was to visualize areas of California where they are most, and least, numerous. This can help identify contiguous areas that may be important to maintain for species viability, such as the length of the Sierra Nevada at upper elevations, the link between the southern Sierra Nevada and the Coast Range, or the areas along major river corridors in the San Joaquin Valley.

Mountain lion (*Puma concolor*)
Photo © Galen Rowell/Mountain Light

Modoc and Sierra Regions

The Modoc Region extends across California's northeast corner from Oregon to Nevada, and south to the southern border of Lassen County. This is a region of forests, mountains, high desert, picturesque valleys, and pine woodlands sparsely populated by humans. The climate features hot, dry summers and cold, moist winters, with snow at higher elevations. Much of this region is volcanic. Western parts of the region contain extensive forests of Jeffrey pine (*Pinus jeffreyi*), white fir (*Abies concolor*), and incense cedar (*Calocedrus decurrens*) studded with lakes and wetlands. Eastern parts are much drier. Shrublands and juniper woodlands dominate, with scattered desert alkali lakes.

The Sierra Region is a vast and rugged mountainous area extending some 380 miles along California's eastern side. It shares spectacular Lake Tahoe with Nevada, features three national parks—Yosemite, Kings Canyon, and Sequoia—and contains 14,495 foot Mount Whitney, the highest peak in the contiguous United States. Summers are dry and mild, and winters are snowy. The mountains support mixed evergreen forests at lower elevations and lodgepole pine (*Pinus contorta*) forests, red fir (*Abies magnifica*) forests, and alpine tundra vegetation at higher altitudes. The vegetation shifts dramatically to arid shrublands on the eastern side of the Sierra, where precipitation decreases drastically.

Marc Hoshovsky

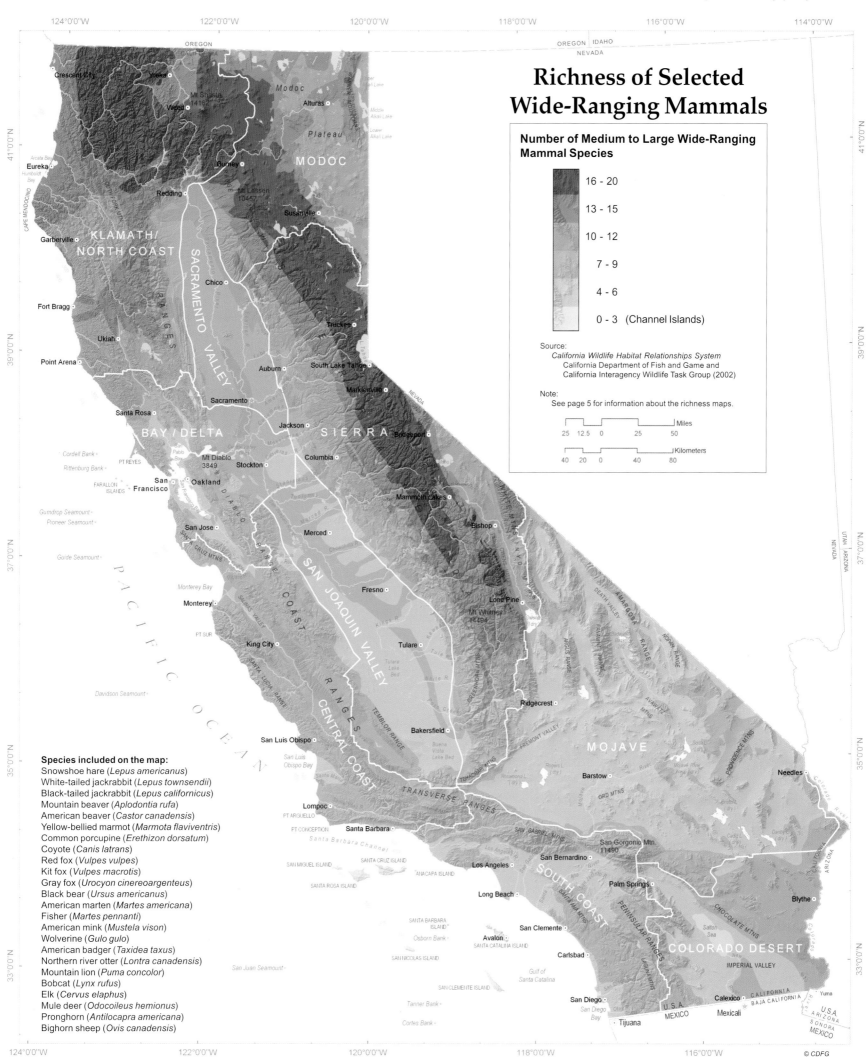

Richness of Selected Wide-Ranging Mammals

Number of Medium to Large Wide-Ranging Mammal Species

16 - 20

13 - 15

10 - 12

7 - 9

4 - 6

0 - 3 (Channel Islands)

Source:
California Wildlife Habitat Relationships System
California Department of Fish and Game and
California Interagency Wildlife Task Group (2002)

Note:
See page 5 for information about the richness maps.

Miles
25 12.5 0   25   50

Kilometers
40   20   0   40   80

Species included on the map:
Snowshoe hare (*Lepus americanus*)
White-tailed jackrabbit (*Lepus townsendii*)
Black-tailed jackrabbit (*Lepus californicus*)
Mountain beaver (*Aplodontia rufa*)
American beaver (*Castor canadensis*)
Yellow-bellied marmot (*Marmota flaviventris*)
Common porcupine (*Erethizon dorsatum*)
Coyote (*Canis latrans*)
Red fox (*Vulpes vulpes*)
Kit fox (*Vulpes macrotis*)
Gray fox (*Urocyon cinereoargenteus*)
Black bear (*Ursus americanus*)
American marten (*Martes americana*)
Fisher (*Martes pennanti*)
American mink (*Mustela vison*)
Wolverine (*Gulo gulo*)
American badger (*Taxidea taxus*)
Northern river otter (*Lontra canadensis*)
Mountain lion (*Puma concolor*)
Bobcat (*Lynx rufus*)
Elk (*Cervus elaphus*)
Mule deer (*Odocoileus hemionus*)
Pronghorn (*Antilocapra americana*)
Bighorn sheep (*Ovis canadensis*)

© CDFG

Freshwater Fishes

By Chuck Knutson

The freshwater fishes of California are represented by 67 native resident and anadromous species (Moyle and Davis 2000). Resident fish spend their entire lives in fresh water while anadromous fish spawn in fresh water and migrate to the ocean as juveniles to grow and mature. The most common native residents are trout, minnows, and suckers. Common anadromous fishes are Chinook salmon (*Oncorhynchus tshawytscha*), steelhead trout (*Oncorhynchus mykiss irideus*), lampreys, and sturgeons.

California roach
(*Lavinia symmetricus*)
Photo © Thomas Taylor

All California freshwater fish species need clean water with sufficient levels of oxygen and water temperatures within their tolerance limits. They need an adequate food supply in the form of detritus, algae, invertebrates, or small fish. Suitable spawning and rearing habitat and, in some cases, cover to protect them from predators are also required.

Prickly sculpin (*Cottus asper*)
Photo © Thomas Taylor

Tahoe sucker (*Catostomus tahoensis*)
Photo © Peter Rissler

Generally, native fish species richness is highest in low elevation rivers and lakes. In the Sacramento Valley and Bay/Delta regions, very high fish species diversity is present because of highly productive aquatic habitat along the Sacramento River, in the estuary where the Sacramento and San Joaquin rivers merge, and in the Suisun Marsh. The desert regions support very few native fishes, although some special status taxa, such as the pupfishes, do exist there.

Green sturgeon
(*Acipenser medirostris*)
Photo: Daniel W. Gotshall

Bay/Delta Region

The Bay/Delta Region includes those counties that border on the San Francisco Bay or the Sacramento-San Joaquin Delta. It is one of the state's most densely populated areas, second only to the South Coast. The region is mostly hilly with low coastal mountains and several peaks rising above 3,000 feet. Oak woodlands and grasslands dominate most of the natural landscape. Coastal salt marsh is found around the San Francisco Bay, and transitions into brackish and then freshwater marsh in the Delta.

Marc Hoshovsky

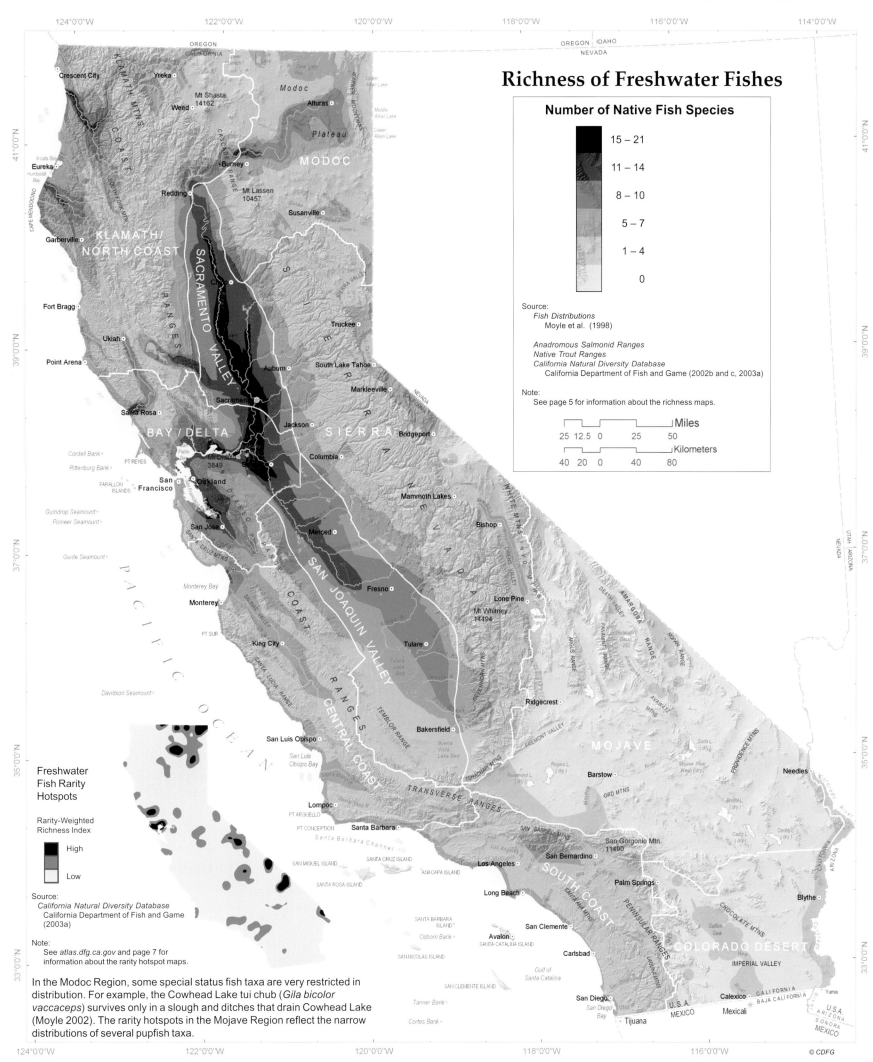

Richness of Freshwater Fishes

Number of Native Fish Species

15 – 21

11 – 14

8 – 10

5 – 7

1 – 4

0

Source:
Fish Distributions
Moyle et al. (1998)

Anadromous Salmonid Ranges
Native Trout Ranges
California Natural Diversity Database
California Department of Fish and Game (2002b and c, 2003a)

Note:
See page 5 for information about the richness maps.

Miles
25 12.5 0   25   50

Kilometers
40 20 0   40   80

Freshwater Fish Rarity Hotspots

Rarity-Weighted
Richness Index

High

Low

Source:
California Natural Diversity Database
California Department of Fish and Game
(2003a)

Note:
See *atlas.dfg.ca.gov* and page 7 for
information about the rarity hotspot maps.

In the Modoc Region, some special status fish taxa are very restricted in
distribution. For example, the Cowhead Lake tui chub (*Gila bicolor
vaccaceps*) survives only in a slough and ditches that drain Cowhead Lake
(Moyle 2002). The rarity hotspots in the Mojave Region reflect the narrow
distributions of several pupfish taxa.

© CDFG

Special Status Invertebrates

By Darlene McGriff

Invertebrates are animals without backbones. They include such diverse groups as worms, mollusks, crustaceans, spiders, and insects. It is estimated that there are about 28,000 species of insects in California. For butterflies alone, the most recent estimate for California is 636 taxa.

Many invertebrate species that were formerly common now have special status because most of their habitat has been destroyed. This is the situation in the Bay/Delta Region. Seven butterfly species were once common in the grassland, coastal dune, and coastal scrub habitats of the San Francisco peninsula. Extensive development over the past 100 years has eliminated most of their habitat. Today, two of the butterflies that lived on the coastal dunes are extinct. A third dune butterfly, Myrtles silverspot butterfly (*Speyeria zerene myrtleae*), is gone from the San Francisco peninsula and can only be found on the dunes in Marin and Sonoma counties. All of the five surviving butterflies are listed by the federal government as threatened or endangered.

The Bay checkerspot butterfly (*Euphydryas editha bayensis*) is one of five surviving special status butterflies of the San Francisco Bay Area.
Photo © Les Junge

Another unique assemblage of special status invertebrates inhabits Antioch Dunes, also in the Bay/Delta Region. This dune system, on the banks of the San Joaquin River by the town of Antioch, was once

Fairy shrimp and tadpole shrimp are the most conspicuous invertebrates of vernal pools, a declining habitat. Vernal pool tadpole shrimp (*Lepidurus packardi*), right, is listed as federally endangered.
Photo © Larry Serpa

home to a rich and varied insect fauna and contained one of the highest concentrations of endemic insects in the United States. Intensive development and sand mining in the 1950s destroyed most of this unique and isolated habitat. Today, the list of extinct endemic California insects known from Antioch Dunes (eight) is longer than the list of surviving endemic insects (five).

In the South Coast Region, another remnant dune system, the El Segundo Dunes, and a mosaic of salt marsh, mudflat, dune, and scrub habitat, the Ballona Wetlands, provide the last remaining habitat for a number of special status invertebrates. These include the federally listed El Segundo blue butterfly (*Euphilotes battoides allyni*), Henne's eucosman moth (*Eucosma hennei*), and Lange's El Segundo dune weevil (*Onychobaris langei*). Five other invertebrates that are found here exist in only a handful of other locations.

Not all special status invertebrates occur in areas in which only habitat fragments remain. A species can also gain special status because it lives exclusively in a specialized or isolated habitat. In the Santa Cruz Mountains, the uplifting and erosion of ancient marine sediments created the Zayante sand hills ecosystem. This unique habitat contains a number of endemic species, including the federally listed Mount Hermon June beetle (*Polyphylla barbata*) and Zayante band-winged grasshopper (*Trimerotropis infantilis*). Another example is found high above timberline in the White Mountains on the California-Nevada border. This remote area is home to several butterfly species, including the White Mountains saepiolus blue butterfly (*Plebejus saepiolus albomontanus*), the White Mountains icarioides blue butterfly (*Icaricia icarioides albihalos*), and the White Mountains skipper (*Hesperia miriamae longaevicola*).

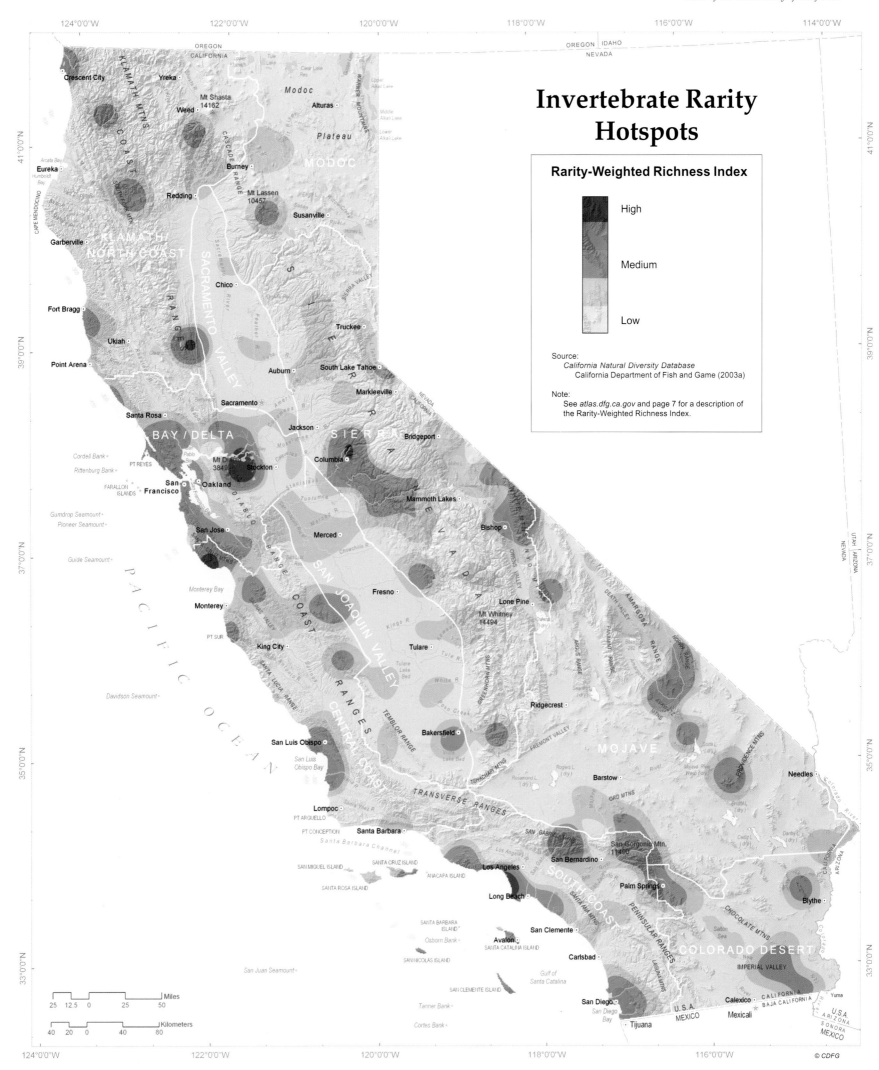

Invertebrate Rarity Hotspots

Rarity-Weighted Richness Index

High

Medium

Low

Source:
California Natural Diversity Database
California Department of Fish and Game (2003a)

Note:
See *atlas.dfg.ca.gov* and page 7 for a description of
the Rarity-Weighted Richness Index.

Samples of Biodiversity

Habitats and Species From Throughout California

Athene cunicularia.

J. TERMER

BURROWING OWL

California supports resources of national and even international significance for biodiversity. Its 1,100 miles of coastline support magnificent kelp forests. Along this coastline, anadromous salmon and trout, many of which are threatened or endangered, return from the ocean to spawn in California's rivers and streams. Coast redwoods are found nowhere else in the world but California and a small portion of Oregon. Valley oak and blue oak, found only at certain elevations above the Sacramento Valley and San Joaquin Valley regions and along the coast, are pure California endemics. The biologically-rich San Francisco Bay and Delta together comprise the largest estuary on the west coast of the United States. The riparian habitat of California's rivers and streams and the grassland habitat found in California's interior are breeding areas for migrating birds from as far away as South America. The state has one of the most extensive distributions of vernal pool habitat known in the world. California is also home to the golden trout, which has evolved over thousands of years in the Kern River drainages of the southern Sierra Nevada. And, in the Mojave Desert, more than 200 of the 1,500 plant taxa and five of the seven pupfish taxa found there are endemic to California.

Kelp Forests

By Larry Espinosa

California kelp, often called seaweed, belongs to the group of marine organisms known as brown algae. Two distinct species of kelp develop broad forest canopies along the shallow, rocky coast. Giant kelp (*Macrocystis pyrifera*) grows abundantly in the state's southern waters and bull kelp (*Nereocystis luetkeana*) grows mostly in the north. In central California, the two species are found side by side.

Giant kelp (*Macrocystis pyrifera*) forest
Photo © Ken Howard

Kelp grows in waters up to 100 feet deep, depending on light penetration. These stately, tree-like plants can grow up to 150 feet when the ocean's climate is optimal. At the surface, they bend over to form broad and dense canopies. For kelp, good environmental conditions include steady currents, penetrating sunlight, and nutrient-rich cool water.

Bull kelp (*Nereocystis luetkeana*)
Photo © Bill Palmer

Giant and bull kelp differ in appearance, geographical distribution, and growth patterns, yet they fulfill the same ecological role. A kelp forest provides a place for fish and invertebrates to grow, live, hide, and eat. Seabirds, marine mammals, and even other rocky-reef plants depend on kelp for food, reproduction, or shelter during a part of their lives. Otters graze on the invertebrates that live on kelp fronds and feed on abalone and sea urchins found at the base of kelp plants. Seals and sea lions feed on small fish that are trying to hide among the kelp fronds. Even "drift kelp," which is made up of fronds and blades that have sloughed off the main plant, provides food for abalone, sea urchins, and other invertebrates as it deteriorates. The rich diversity of the kelp environment along California's nearshore coastline provides exciting opportunities for divers, anglers, and underwater photographers.

In addition to periodic changes in the ocean's climate, human disturbances have affected kelp over the past 20 years. Sewage effluents, shoreline erosion, and power plant discharges are some of the factors that have caused long term declines in California kelp productivity. Regrowth has resulted from natural factors and restoration efforts.

Because kelp provides important habitat for many marine species, while serving recreational needs and commercial demands for industrial and food products, it is a key living marine resource. For this reason, special regulations govern the manner in which kelp is harvested. Managing kelp to balance its availability for all of its uses is a challenge for stewards of ocean life.

Sea otters (*Enhydra lutris*) feed on invertebrates that live in kelp forests.
They commonly form resting groups, or rafts, in kelp canopies.
Photo © Ken Howard

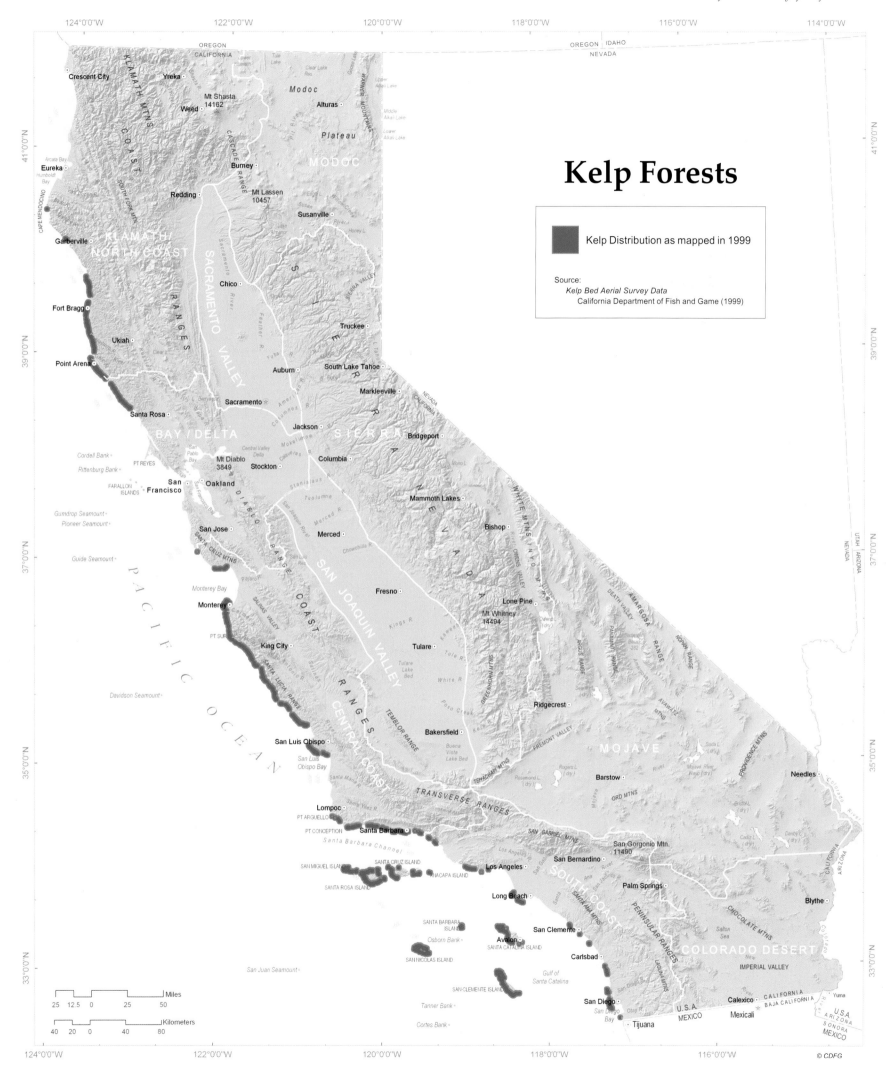

Kelp Forests

Kelp Distribution as mapped in 1999

Source:
Kelp Bed Aerial Survey Data
California Department of Fish and Game (1999)

Anadromous Salmonids

By Ronald Rogers

Juvenile Chinook salmon
(*Oncorhynchus
tshawytscha*)
Photo © John Hannon

Anadromous salmon and trout species are an important biological resource of California. The most abundant of these are Chinook (king) salmon (*Oncorhynchus tshawytscha*), coho (silver) salmon (*O. kisutch*), and coastal rainbow trout/steelhead (*O. mykiss irideus*). Coastal cutthroat trout (*O. clarki clarki*) are less abundant. Pink salmon (*O. gorbuscha*), chum salmon (*O. keta*), and sockeye salmon (*O. nerka*) may also occasionally be found in California streams, but they do not maintain self-sustaining populations. Long before European settlers arrived, some Native American cultures depended upon these abundant resources. Since the 1850's, major commercial and sport fisheries have existed for these fish, leading to high public interest in their conservation.

Anadromous salmon and trout hatch in freshwater streams and live there from a few weeks to over a year before migrating to the ocean. These fish typically mature in the ocean and then return to their home streams as three- to five-year olds to reproduce. Highly developed olfactory senses and visual cues guide them there. Streams with clean gravel in cool, well-oxygenated water are required for the fish to build nests or "redds" and cover their eggs for protection until the eggs can hatch and emerge from the gravel as "fry." Cool summer water temperatures, often found only in the headwaters of streams, are required for survival of these young fish. When adults return to their home stream to spawn, the group of fish and the event is known as a "run." Salmon die after spawning, but steelhead and coastal cutthroat trout can live to repeat the cycle.

Major Chinook runs occur in the large rivers of the Central Valley, the Klamath River and its major tributaries, and, to a lesser extent, the other rivers of the north coast. From Oregon to Monterey, watersheds of the coast supply the necessary conditions for coho salmon. Because the young spend at least a year in fresh water before migrating to sea, they need cool summer water temperatures to survive and grow. Steelhead may be found wherever salmon are, but range further south along the entire California coast and also move higher into the headwaters of streams. Coastal cutthroat trout live from the Eel River north. The other three salmon—pink, chum, and sockeye—sometimes occupy the Sacramento River and various north coast streams.

Since the late 19th century, salmon and steelhead have taken heavy losses from destruction of habitat and over-fishing. Ambitious water and power projects have left all the major rivers of the state with dams, blocking fish migration. Major water diversions, watershed erosion, and pollution have destroyed or degraded habitat. Even with fish hatcheries, salmon and steelhead numbers have continued to decline and certain major runs have been eliminated or are nearing extinction.

Maintaining water flows and water quality and continuing to manage fishing activities remain important to the conservation of salmonid species. In the long term, managing genetic diversity is just as important. This includes restoring both habitat and the local genetic stocks of fish uniquely adapted to occupy that habitat. Small, isolated fish populations must also be protected because they are genetically unique and thus contribute to diversity. In addition, government and private citizens and organizations, working cooperatively, can preserve the salmonid contribution to California's biodiversity.

Spawning coho salmon
(*Oncorhynchus kisutch*) on
the North Fork Elk River,
Klamath/North Coast Region
DFG Photo: Allan Renger

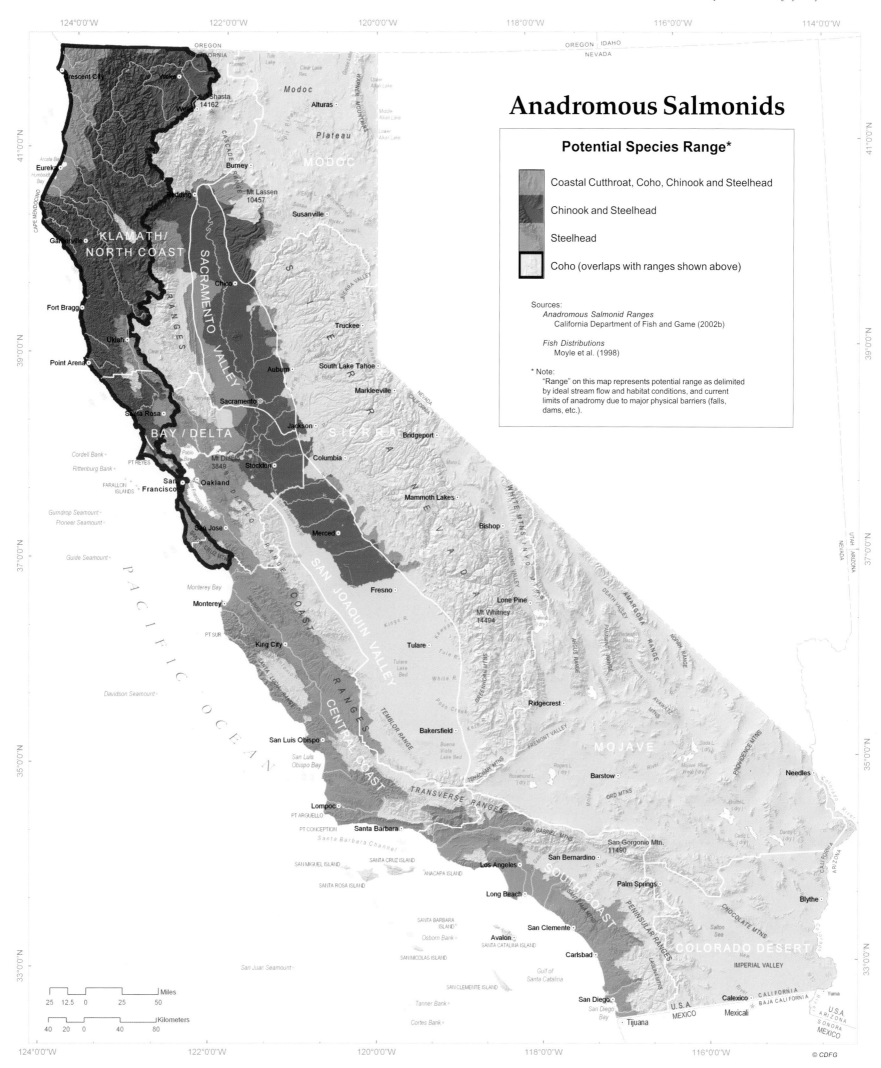

Anadromous Salmonids

Potential Species Range*

Coastal Cutthroat, Coho, Chinook and Steelhead

Chinook and Steelhead

Steelhead

Coho (overlaps with ranges shown above)

Sources:
Anadromous Salmonid Ranges
California Department of Fish and Game (2002b)

Fish Distributions
Moyle et al. (1998)

* Note:
"Range" on this map represents potential range as delimited
by ideal stream flow and habitat conditions, and current
limits of anadromy due to major physical barriers (falls,
dams, etc.).

© CDFG

Coast Redwoods

By Esther Burkett

A magnificent contribution to the biodiversity of California is the coast redwood (*Sequoia sempervirens*), known as the world's tallest living tree. Many visitors are awestruck when standing amid old growth giants towering well over 300 feet skyward, with huge bases ranging in diameter from 10 to 25 feet.

Redwoods are remarkably adapted to sprouting new growth after falling, burning, or being cut. Fallen trees even serve as "nursery logs" where seedlings begin their growth in the deep, moist furrows of the long-lasting bark. Redwoods are also extremely long lived. In old growth forests, the average age is about 600 years, with a few trees exceeding 1,500 years.

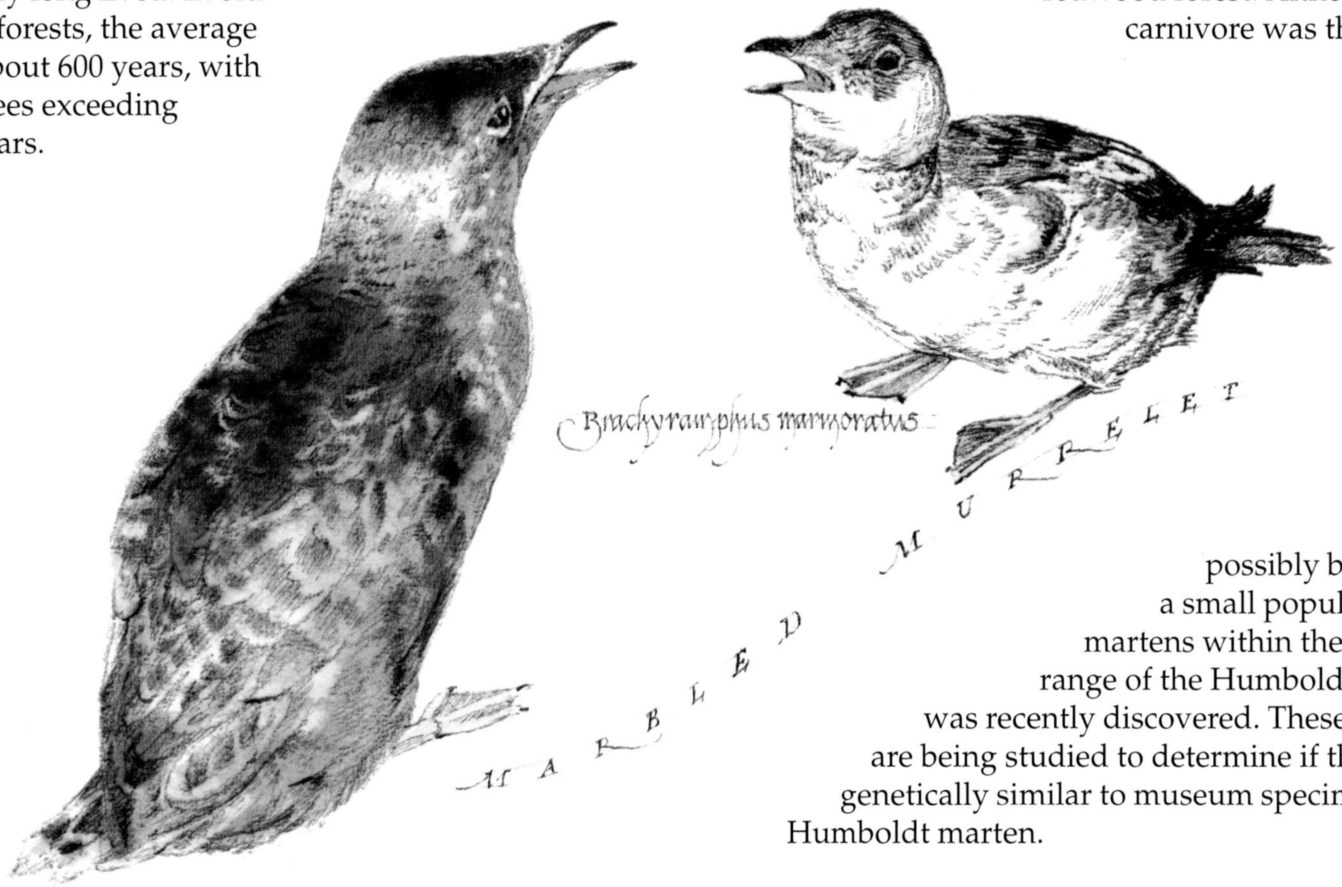

Some animals occur in higher densities in old growth redwoods than in harvested redwood forests. Examples include Marbled Murrelet (*Brachyramphus marmoratus*), an endangered seabird that nests in redwoods; southern torrent salamander (*Rhyacotriton variegatus)*; and tailed frog (*Ascaphus truei*). Studies of these animals are ongoing in an attempt to further understand their habitat needs and promote their conservation.

The Humboldt marten (*Martes americana humboldtensis*) may have been largely endemic to the redwood forest. Although this carnivore was thought to

Brachyramphus marmoratus

MARBLED MURRELET

possibly be extinct, a small population of martens within the historic range of the Humboldt marten was recently discovered. These animals are being studied to determine if they are genetically similar to museum specimens of Humboldt marten.

Coast redwood forest is found only along the coast from southern Oregon to Monterey County. Coastal fog helps provide critical moisture during the drier summer months. Strong winds off major points such as Cape Mendocino and Point Reyes disperse the fog, causing "wind gaps." This is one theory to account for the discontinuous distribution of redwoods along the coast.

Today, it is estimated that approximately four percent of the largest old growth redwood forests remain. Two keys to the long term viability of the coast redwood ecosystem are the regrowth of logged areas in park lands and private timber lands, and the practices of sustainable forestry and stream protection. Given the fast growth rate of redwoods and their remarkable sprouting abilities, the biodiversity of the forest can be secured with careful management.

Coast Redwoods

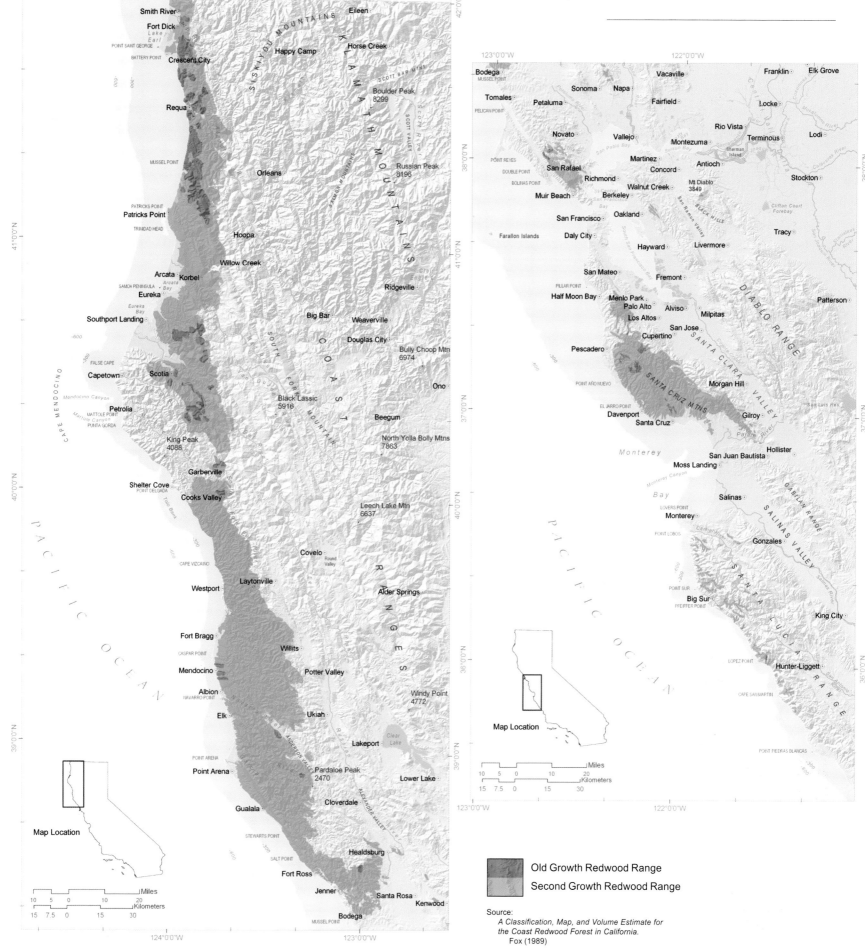

Old Growth Redwood Range

Second Growth Redwood Range

Source:
A Classification, Map, and Volume Estimate for the Coast Redwood Forest in California.
Fox (1989)

© CDFG

Oak Woodlands

By Barrett Garrison

Oak woodlands are one of California's most characteristic wildlife habitats. Scattered oak trees, green or golden brown grass, grazing cattle, and ranch houses and barns on gently rolling hills are typical scenes for many Californians traveling the state's country roads and highways. Oak woodlands occupy approximately 10 million acres or 10 percent of the state. These woodlands form rings in and around the larger inland valleys and coastal regions.

Oak woodland
DFG photo: Todd Keeler-Wolf

Woodlands are mostly a mixture of trees and grasses, but other types of herbaceous vegetation and shrubs also occur. They are distinguished from forests based on the number of trees and the amount of canopy; woodlands have more open canopy than forests. Although there are 18 different species of oak in California, the state's oak woodlands are dominated by five of them: blue (*Quercus douglasii*), valley (*Q. lobata*), coast live (*Q. agrifolia*), interior live (*Q. wislizenii*), and Engelmann (*Q. engelmannii*) oak.

Western Scrub-Jay (*Aphelocoma californica*)
with acorn
Photo © Willy Cowell

Oaks belong to the plant genus *Quercus*, a Latin word derived from two Celtic words—*quer*, meaning fine, and *cuez*, meaning tree. The oaks in California range from short, ground-hugging shrubs to large, stately trees. Oaks have some unique characteristics. The fruit is a hard

The Acorn Woodpecker (*Melanerpes formicivorus*) derives its name from its acorn collecting habits.
Photo © Timothy Floyd

nut known as an acorn. The distinctive flowers are wind pollinated. Oaks are also long-lived plants, with some trees living for centuries. The wood is very strong. Oaks occur throughout the world but oak woodlands typically occur only in areas with Mediterranean climates that characteristically have cool, wet winters and hot, dry summers.

Oak woodlands support a large number of plant and animal species. Some 5,000 species of insects; more than 330 species of amphibians, reptiles, birds, and mammals; and several thousand plant species live in these woodlands. Some of California's most characteristic wildlife, including Acorn Woodpecker (*Melanerpes formicivorus*), mule deer (*Odocoileus hemionus*), mountain lion (*Puma concolor*), California Quail (*Callipepla californica*), Western Scrub-Jay (*Aphelocoma californica*), and western gray squirrel (*Sciurus griseus*) are found in these habitats. Approximately 50 species of birds and mammals eat acorns, an important value of oak woodlands to the state's wildlife.

California Quail
(*Callipepla californica*)
Photo © John C. Muegge

Because of their beauty, favorable climates, and location, California's oak woodlands are desirable places for houses, golf courses, businesses, vineyards, and orchards. Oak woodlands are being reduced by these developments. Habitat is also being modified by the cutting of oaks for firewood. All Californians should carefully consider the long term effects of various land use practices if we are to conserve oak woodlands for future generations.

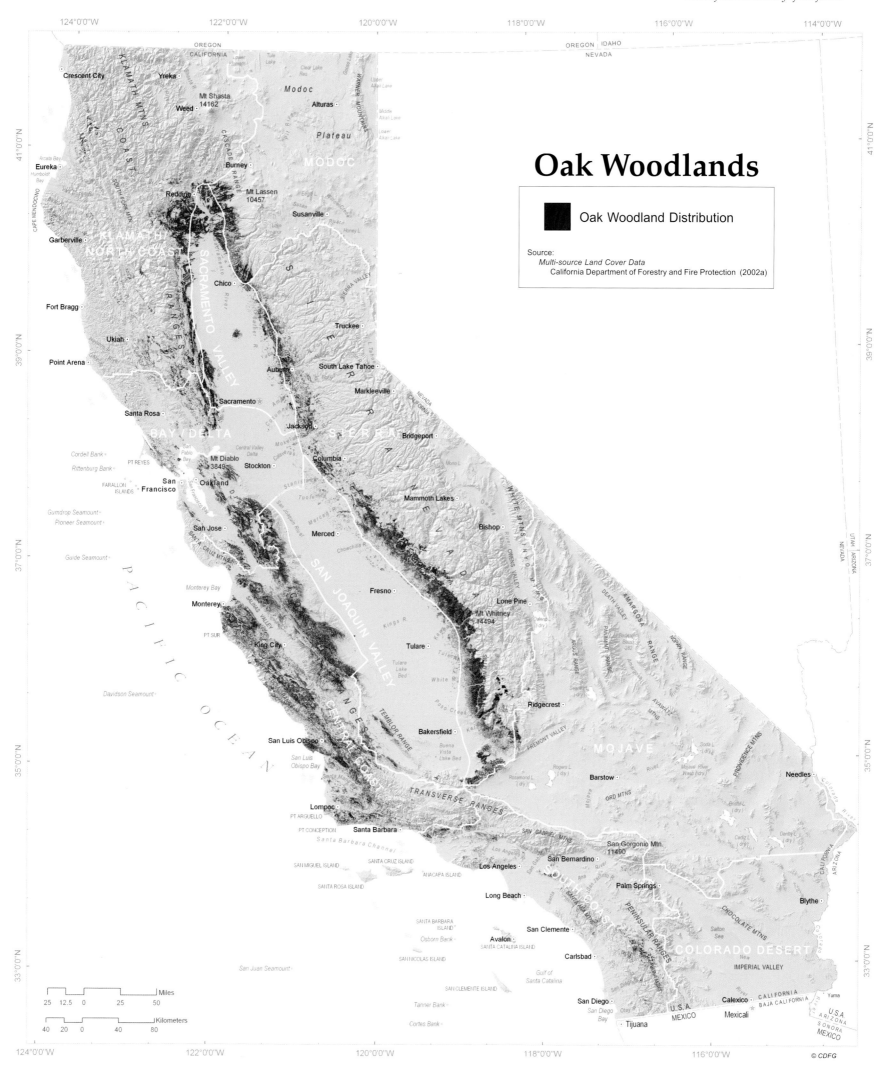

Oak Woodlands

■ Oak Woodland Distribution

Source:
Multi-source Land Cover Data
California Department of Forestry and Fire Protection (2002a)

Riparian Habitat

By Scott Clemons

Riparian habitat includes the trees, other vegetation, and physical features normally found on the banks and floodplains of rivers, streams, and other bodies of fresh water. Although riparian areas occupy a very small part of the total land area in the state, they support a tremendous number of fish and wildlife species. Over 225 species of birds, mammals, reptiles, and amphibians depend upon California's riparian habitats

Riparian habitat,
Diablo Range,
Bay/Delta Region
Photo © Ed Ely

(Knopf et al. 1988, Saab et al. 1995, Dobkin et al. 1998). In addition, these beautiful examples of California's biodiversity can help reduce flood flows and flood damage, improve groundwater recharge, prevent damaging chemicals and other compounds from reaching open water, and reduce wind and erosion on adjacent lands.

In July of 1841, William Dane Phelps traveled up the Sacramento River to visit Captain Sutter, and was impressed by (as quoted in Warner and Hendrix 1984) "...the immense size of the trees, the dense thickness of the unpenetrated forests in some places, and the level plains with here and there a bunch of scrub oaks without underbrush in others, together with a

Wilson's Warbler (*Wilsonia pusilla*)
Photo © James Gallagher

profusion of wild flowers...a beautiful gently undulating country abiding with rich feed and agreeably diversified with trees & wild shrubbery." This is a vivid example of the luxuriant riparian habitat conditions that existed before extensive modification by European settlement.

Unfortunately, human activities have destroyed or fragmented most of this valuable habitat over the past 150 years. No one has documented how much riparian habitat existed in California before 1850. However, a 1984 study estimated that riparian vegetation in the Central Valley and desert regions represented from two percent to five percent of the pre-1850 amount. The northern coastal streams still support up to 15 percent of their pre-1850 riparian vegetation (Katibah 1984). Because they are both biologically rich and severely degraded, riparian areas have been identified as the most critical habitat for conserving neotropical migrant birds. These are birds that spend the winter in the tropical parts of the Western Hemisphere and the breeding season here in California (Miller 1951, Gaines 1974, Manley and Davidson 1993).

Riparian vegetation, San Joaquin River, San Joaquin Valley Region
State Lands Commission photo: Diana Jacobs

During the last few decades many resource agencies and conservation organizations have worked cooperatively on public and private land to protect, enhance, and restore riparian habitats. Many of the Golden State's wildlife resources depend upon our continued dedication to restoring this habitat to the healthiest quality and largest extent possible.

Riparian habitat, Stanislaus River,
Bay/Delta Region
DFG photo: Todd Keeler-Wolf

Riparian Habitat

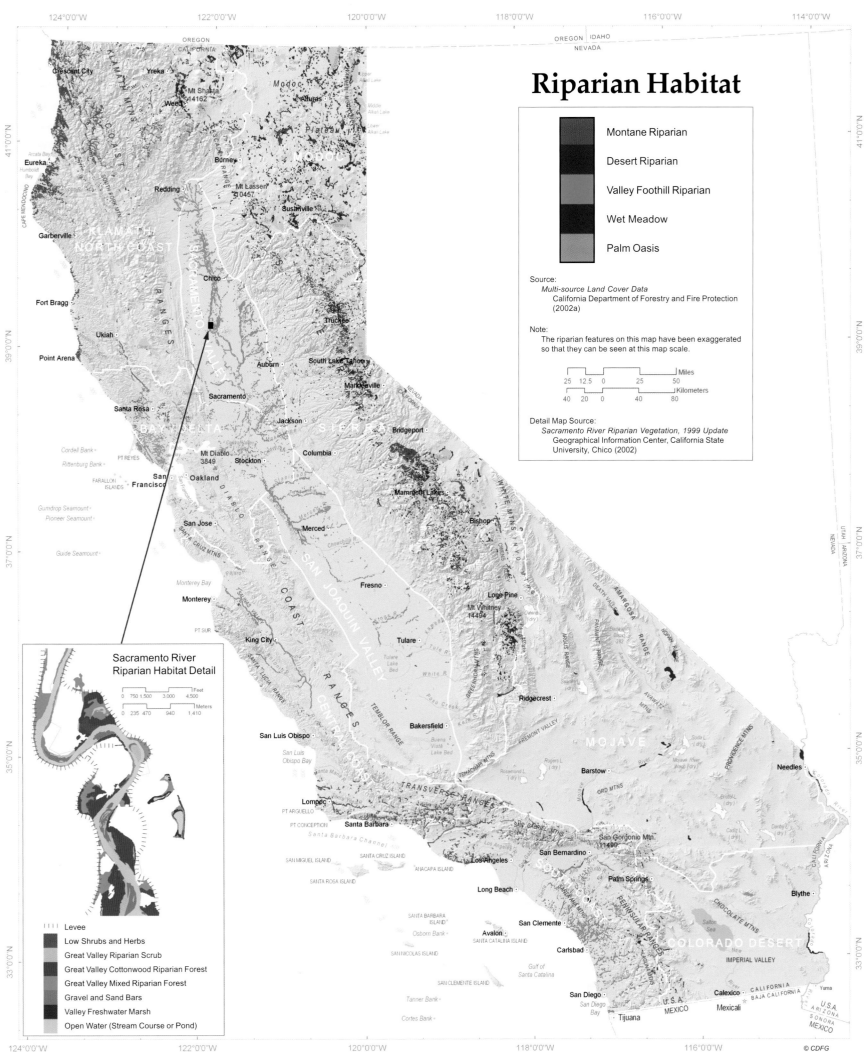

Legend:

- Montane Riparian
- Desert Riparian
- Valley Foothill Riparian
- Wet Meadow
- Palm Oasis

Source:
Multi-source Land Cover Data
California Department of Forestry and Fire Protection
(2002a)

Note:
The riparian features on this map have been exaggerated
so that they can be seen at this map scale.

Detail Map Source:
Sacramento River Riparian Vegetation, 1999 Update
Geographical Information Center, California State
University, Chico (2002)

Sacramento River Riparian Habitat Detail

- ||||| Levee
- Low Shrubs and Herbs
- Great Valley Riparian Scrub
- Great Valley Cottonwood Riparian Forest
- Great Valley Mixed Riparian Forest
- Gravel and Sand Bars
- Valley Freshwater Marsh
- Open Water (Stream Course or Pond)

© CDFG

Bay-Delta Wetlands

By Eric Kauffman

"Wetland" is a general term referring to the transitional zone between aquatic and terrestrial (or upland) areas. The water table is usually at or near the surface, or the land is covered by shallow water for at least a portion of the year. Wetlands are a highly productive source of food, supporting a vast array of plants and animals, many of them microscopic. They also filter certain sediments and pollutants that otherwise would be released into open water.

Salt marsh at China Camp State Park, Bay/Delta Region
Photo © Brenda Grewell

Wetlands occur throughout California in many different forms. They include brackish intertidal wetlands along the coast, riparian wetlands along rivers and streams, freshwater marshes at the edges of lakes, and vernal pools within grasslands in many parts of the state.

California's most extensive network of wetlands can be found along the riverbanks, sloughs, shallow ponds, and mudflats of the Bay/ Delta Region. More than a dozen major rivers flow into the Central Valley from the Sierra, Cascade, Klamath, and Coast Ranges. Most of these converge in the Delta, a network of slow-running sloughs spanning an area from Sacramento to south of Stockton. The Delta then empties into

Salt marsh, Bay/Delta Region
Photo © Brian O'Neill

American Avocet (*Recurvirostra americana*) in mudflats, Bay/Delta Region
Photo © Don Moore

Suisun Bay. Other rivers and creeks, such as the Napa River and Petaluma River in the north, and Stevens, Coyote, and Alamitos creeks in the south, flow directly into the greater San Francisco Bay. Lining the edge of the bay system are mudflats that are submerged and exposed with each rise and fall of the tides.

Much of this network of sloughs, river channels, and mudflats is estuarine, meaning a mix of sea water and fresh water. It is also intertidal, being influenced by the rise and fall of water levels with the ocean tides. Estuaries are extremely productive ecosystems. The mixing of fresh and salt water provides nutrient-rich water for algae, which forms the base of the aquatic food chain. This abundance of algae is food for microscopic animals, or zooplankton, which are food for a host of larger invertebrates, which are in turn eaten by larger animals.

Snowy Egret (*Egretta thula*) in brackish marsh, Bay/Delta Region
Photo © Department of Water Resources

More than 200 species of birds, mammals, reptiles, and amphibians and more than 20 species of freshwater fish are estimated to use the wetlands and aquatic components of the San Francisco Bay and Delta during various times of the year. The size and productivity of the wetlands of the Bay/Delta Region make them a critical component in sustaining the biodiversity of California.

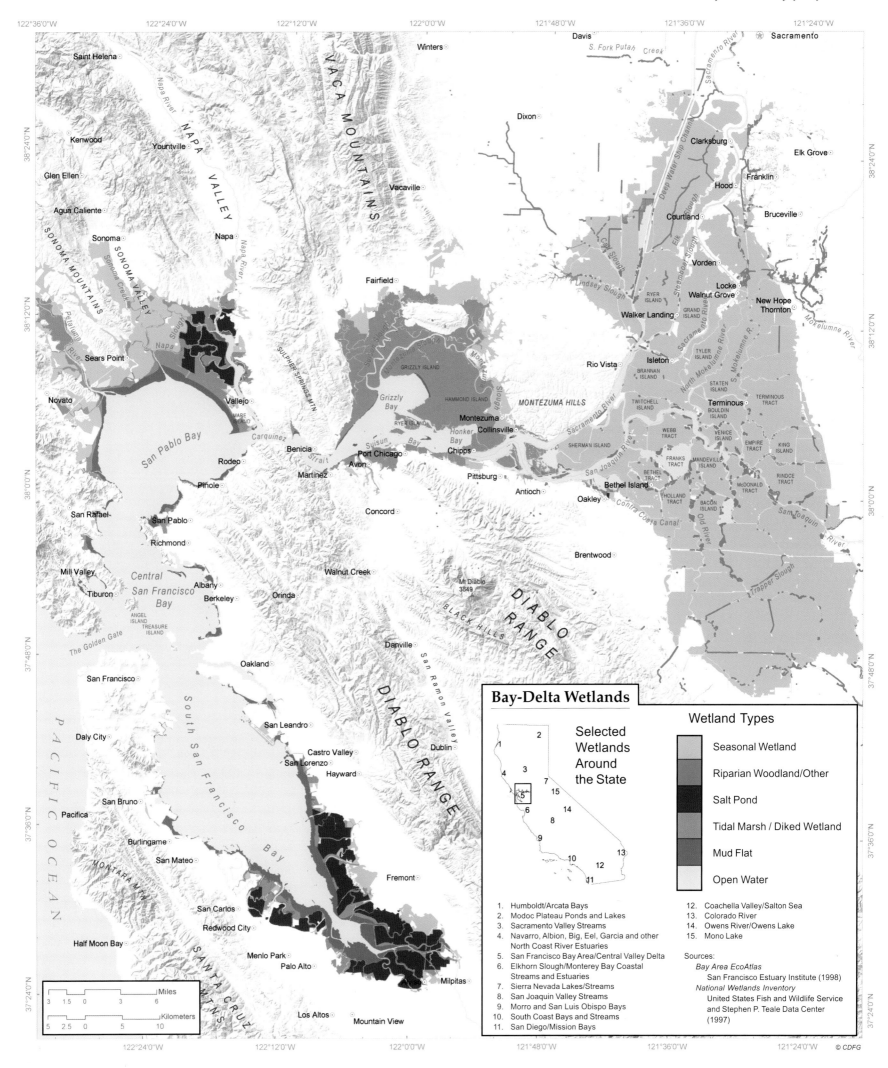

Bay-Delta Wetlands

Selected Wetlands Around the State

Wetland Types

- Seasonal Wetland
- Riparian Woodland/Other
- Salt Pond
- Tidal Marsh / Diked Wetland
- Mud Flat
- Open Water

1. Humboldt/Arcata Bays
2. Modoc Plateau Ponds and Lakes
3. Sacramento Valley Streams
4. Navarro, Albion, Big, Eel, Garcia and other North Coast River Estuaries
5. San Francisco Bay Area/Central Valley Delta
6. Elkhorn Slough/Monterey Bay Coastal Streams and Estuaries
7. Sierra Nevada Lakes/Streams
8. San Joaquin Valley Streams
9. Morro and San Luis Obispo Bays
10. South Coast Bays and Streams
11. San Diego/Mission Bays
12. Coachella Valley/Salton Sea
13. Colorado River
14. Owens River/Owens Lake
15. Mono Lake

Sources:
Bay Area EcoAtlas
San Francisco Estuary Institute (1998)
National Wetlands Inventory
United States Fish and Wildlife Service and Stephen P. Teale Data Center (1997)

© CDFG

Central Valley Grassland Habitat

By Kevin Hunting

Tri-colored Blackbird (*Agelaius tricolor*) with grasshoppers
Photo © Bill Hamilton

The grasslands of California's Central Valley are a unique part of the state's natural heritage. Much like the once extensive Great Plains and prairie habitats of the Midwest and Intermountain West, these grasslands support a highly adapted suite of vegetation types and wildlife species. Although native plant species richness is relatively low in the Sacramento Valley and San Joaquin Valley regions, these areas support among the highest diversity of native freshwater fishes, winter birds, and waterfowl. (See section entitled "Measures of Biodiversity: Richness, Rarity, and Endemism.")

Central Valley grasslands typically occur in relatively level terrain at low elevations—an ideal setting for urban, industrial, and agricultural development. Prior to European settlement, California supported about 22 million acres of grasslands, with about 20 percent occurring in the Central Valley (Huenneke 1989). Today, based on analysis of land cover data, less than 10% of the Valley's grasslands remain (CDF 2002a). Conversion of grassland habitats to urban and agricultural uses has proportionately exceeded conversion of any other habitat in the state (Ewing et al. 1988).

As a consequence of this tremendous loss, many grassland-dependent bird and mammal species have experienced population declines that continue today (Knopf 1995). For species lacking historical population data, declines are inferred from the loss of essential habitat. However, for other species, population trend can be directly measured using long-term monitoring data. For example, the nationwide Breeding Bird Survey, currently managed by the Biological Resources

Division of the United States Geological Survey, stores over 40 years of information about breeding birds in North America. This information is particularly valuable because data have been collected over a long period of time and in a consistent manner, making it possible to produce reliable population trend estimates in many cases. Analysis of the Breeding Bird Survey shows that the populations of grassland-adapted bird species have declined by a larger margin and more steeply than the populations of any other habitat-based group of bird species (for example, forest-adapted or chaparral-adapted species).

San Joaquin antelope squirrels (*Ammospermophilus nelsoni*)
Photo © Peter L. Knapp

Several bird and mammal taxa adapted to Central Valley grasslands have experienced population declines. Most notably, the Mountain Plover (*Charadrius montanus*) and Tri-colored Blackbird (*Agelauis tricolor*) are seasonally near-endemic to California and dependent on grasslands for stable populations. The San Joaquin kit fox (*Vulpes macrotis mutica*), San Joaquin antelope squirrel (*Ammospermophilus nelsoni*), and some subspecies of kangaroo rats (*Dipodomys* spp.) are examples of grassland mammals near-endemic to the Central Valley whose populations are declining. To stem declines and stabilize populations, it is imperative that conservation planning efforts in Central Valley grasslands consider the habitat needs and locations of these birds and mammals.

Mountain Plover
(*Charadrius montanus*)
Photo: Fritz Knopf

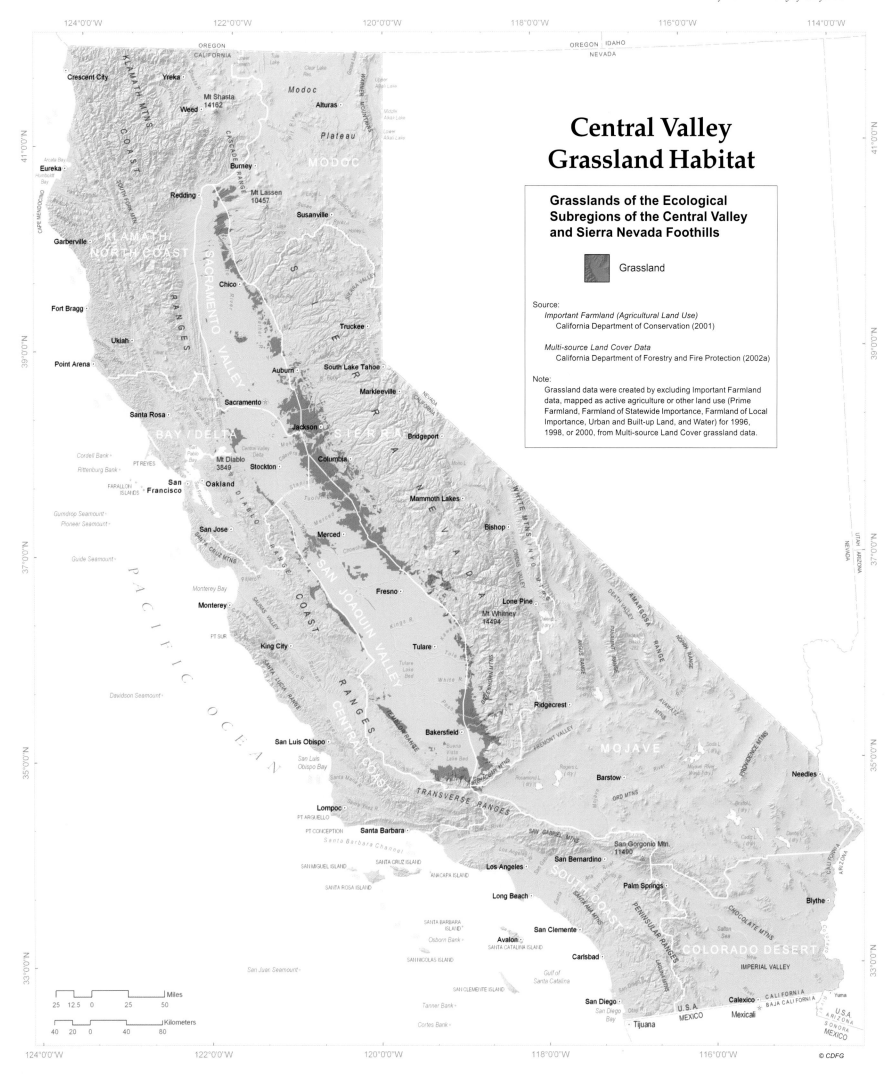

Central Valley Grassland Habitat

Grasslands of the Ecological Subregions of the Central Valley and Sierra Nevada Foothills

Grassland

Source:
Important Farmland (Agricultural Land Use)
California Department of Conservation (2001)

Multi-source Land Cover Data
California Department of Forestry and Fire Protection (2002a)

Note:
Grassland data were created by excluding Important Farmland data, mapped as active agriculture or other land use (Prime Farmland, Farmland of Statewide Importance, Farmland of Local Importance, Urban and Built-up Land, and Water) for 1996, 1998, or 2000, from Multi-source Land Cover grassland data.

© CDFG

Central Valley Vernal Pools

By Kari Lewis

Vernal pools are seasonal wetlands that form in depressions in the soil surface. Because these depressions occur over an impermeable soil or rock layer, they hold rainwater longer than the surrounding terrain—long enough for unique plants and animals to thrive there. Vernal pools are known to occur in parts of the world that, like California, have a Mediterranean climate with areas of impermeable subsurface layers. Other parts of the world where vernal pools are known to occur include Chile and Western Australia.

Vernal pool at Thomes Creek Ecological Reserve,
Sacramento Valley Region
Photo: Carol W. Witham

Vernal pool landscape,
San Joaquin Valley Region
DFG File Photo

California has one of the most extensive distributions of vernal pools known in the world. Vernal pools occur in a majority of the state's regions, from the Modoc Plateau in the northeast to the mesas of the south coast near San Diego (see inset map). The large map at right features the distribution of vernal pool habitat in the Central Valley.

Vernal pools support plants and animals adapted to unique living conditions, which range from very wet to very dry each year. In the winter, pools become the watery home of shrimp, toads, and aquatic plants. In the spring, as the water begins to recede, colorful wildflowers bloom and attract ground dwelling pollinator bees from the uplands nearby. As summer approaches, the pools begin to dry out. Plants tolerant of drier conditions emerge, tree frogs forage, dried eggs of fairy and tadpole shrimp fall into cracks in the mud, and spadefoot toads take to their burrows to await the next winter rains.

It is estimated that California's Central Valley alone once had 4 million acres of vernal pool habitat, which includes the pools themselves and the uplands around them. Today the Central Valley supports just under 1 million acres of vernal pool habitat. This loss of vernal pool habitat is largely attributed to urban development and farming, which continue to threaten California's remaining vernal pools.

Vernal pool Indian paintbrush, bristled downingia, and tricolored monkeyflower
(*Castilleja campestris, Downingia bicornuta, Mimulus tricolor*)
Photo: John Game

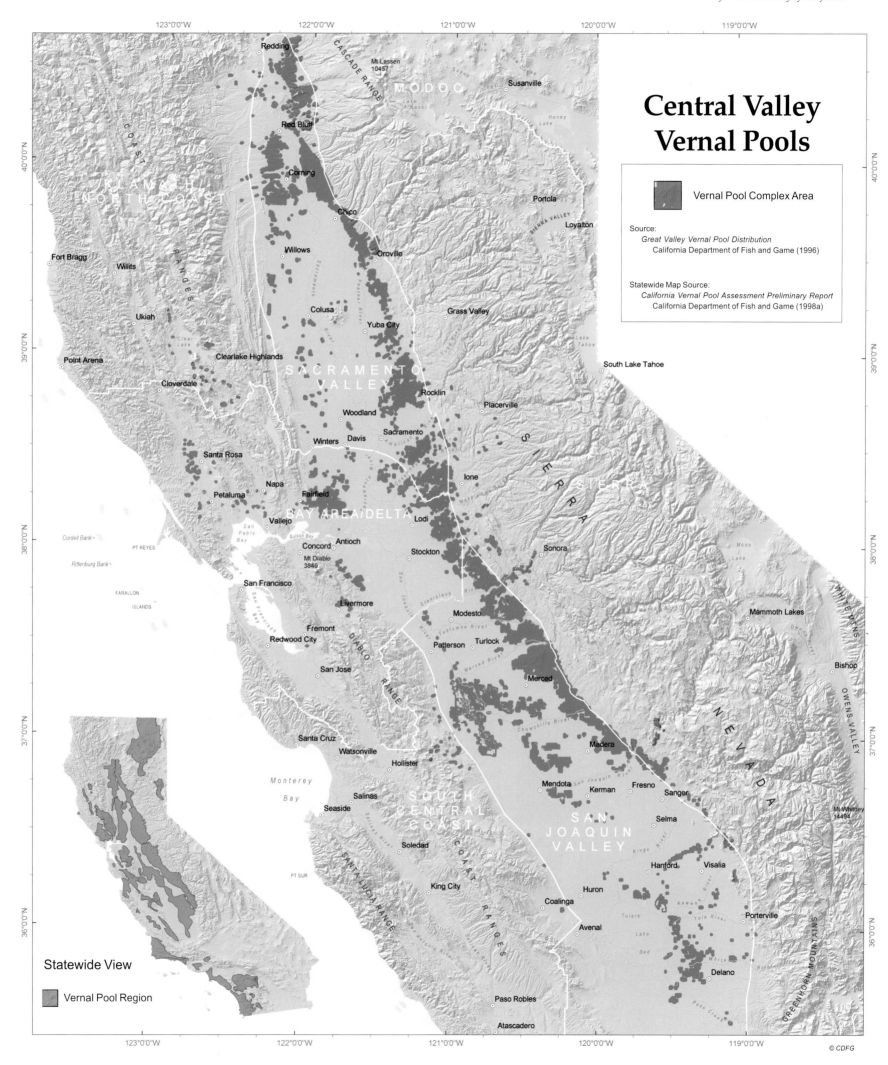

Central Valley Vernal Pools

▨ Vernal Pool Complex Area

Source:
Great Valley Vernal Pool Distribution
California Department of Fish and Game (1996)

Statewide Map Source:
California Vernal Pool Assessment Preliminary Report
California Department of Fish and Game (1998a)

Statewide View

▨ Vernal Pool Region

© CDFG

Trout

By Chuck Knutson and Joe Pisciotto

California supports 11 native trout taxa, including our state fish, the California golden trout (*Oncorhynchus mykiss aguabonita*), considered by many to be the most beautifully-colored trout in the world.

The most common native trout in California is the coastal rainbow trout (*O. m. irideus*), which ranges along the whole coastline of California and through the Cascade Range to the western slope of the Sierra Nevada. Coastal rainbow can be either resident, living in fresh water throughout their life span, or anadromous, going to sea as juveniles to mature and return back to fresh water as steelhead trout to spawn.

Coastal rainbow/steelhead trout coexisted at one time with some of the redband trout varieties in California. Historically, they occupied most of the perennially flowing streams of the Sacramento-San Joaquin valley drainages, and most of California's coastal streams. Their range was limited by barriers such as waterfalls or other impassable obstructions. Some of these barriers would change with time, allowing periodic access to unoccupied habitat or to headwaters where isolated trout populations existed. Here is where coastal rainbow/steelhead are thought to have mixed with redband trout.

Isolated populations of trout such as the state fish, the California golden trout (*Oncorhynchus mykiss aguabonita*), developed color variation unique to their geographic areas.
DFG photo: Curtis Milliron

Kern River trout taxa are thought to have evolved from ancestral stocks of redband trout that occupied the Sacramento and San Joaquin valleys and extended high into the drainages prior to the invasion by rainbow trout. Kern River trout subspecies are believed to have been isolated in stages. The first wave of primitive redband trout moved up into the Kern River drainage before the last ice age. Shortly thereafter, barriers prevented any further invasion of redband trout, and later of rainbow trout, to the upper Kern River. This area is where the California golden trout (*O. m. aguabonita*), the Little Kern golden trout (*O. m. whitei*), and the Kern River rainbow trout (*O. m. gilberti*) evolved.

Lahontan cutthroat trout (*O. clarki henshawi*) are naturally found on the east side of the Sierra. These fish evolved in what was once a huge body of water called Lake Lahontan. Their native ranges are the Truckee, Carson, and Walker drainages. Due to human influences, these fish have vanished from much of their historic range. The Paiute cutthroat trout (*O. c. seleniris*) evolved from the Lahontan cutthroat trout in the upper reaches of Silver King Creek in the Carson River drainage.

California native trout require relatively cool, clear, well-oxygenated water to survive. Invertebrates or small-size forage fish and cover must be abundant to support healthy trout populations. Spawning gravels must be mostly free of fine sediment. Fish must not be blocked from spawning and rearing areas or diverted from streams or lakes into unsuitable habitat. They must be protected from introduced fish species, which cause unnatural competition and interbreeding. California golden trout, like many other isolated populations of trout, have evolved without competition, do very poorly with it, and hybridize with introduced rainbow trout.

Efforts to maintain or increase the distribution and diversity of native trout occur throughout the state. They involve protecting or relocating small remnant populations and establishing new populations.

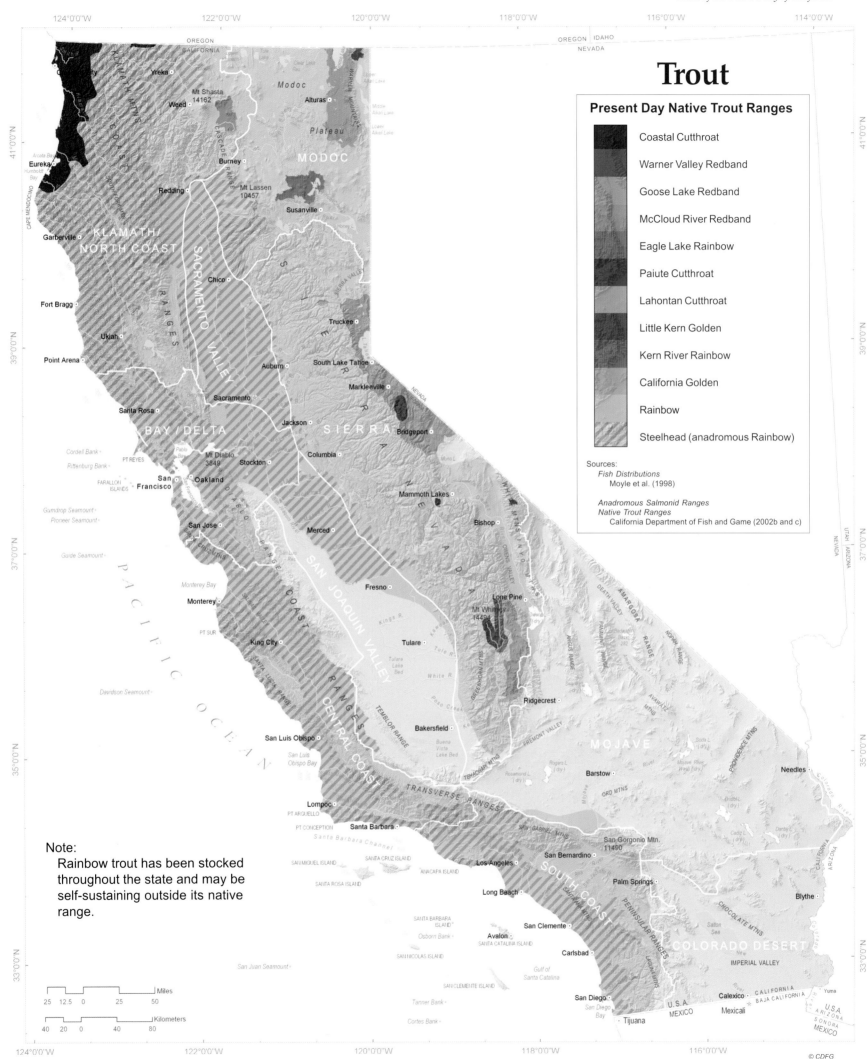

Trout

Present Day Native Trout Ranges

Coastal Cutthroat

Warner Valley Redband

Goose Lake Redband

McCloud River Redband

Eagle Lake Rainbow

Paiute Cutthroat

Lahontan Cutthroat

Little Kern Golden

Kern River Rainbow

California Golden

Rainbow

Steelhead (anadromous Rainbow)

Sources:
Fish Distributions
Moyle et al. (1998)

Anadromous Salmonid Ranges
Native Trout Ranges
California Department of Fish and Game (2002b and c)

Note:
Rainbow trout has been stocked throughout the state and may be self-sustaining outside its native range.

© CDFG

Mojave Desert Vegetation

By Todd Keeler-Wolf

Although considered the smallest North American desert, the Mojave Desert is the largest desert in California. It stretches over approximately one fifth of the state and beyond to southwestern Utah and northwestern Arizona. It epitomizes much of what we consider to be the true desert of the American southwest. Home to such desert icons as the Joshua tree (*Yucca brevifolia*), Death Valley, and the lower reaches of the Grand Canyon of the Colorado River, the Mojave Desert is rich and varied, known for its stark beauty, rugged topography, and high biological diversity. There are an estimated 1,500 plant taxa in the Mojave, 210 of them endemic to the state.

Joshua tree alliance
(*Yucca brevifolia/Pleuraphis rigida* association)
Joshua Tree National Park, Mojave Region
DFG photo: Todd Keeler-Wolf

The Mojave is a transitional desert, lying midway between the hot Sonoran Desert to the south and the cool Great Basin Desert to the north. The pattern of rain and snowfall transitions from a summer-dry pattern reflecting California's Mediterranean climate in the western Mojave to a pattern of winter and summer moisture in the eastern Mojave. Certain succulents such as Utah agave (*Agave utahensis*), Spanish bayonet (*Yucca baccata*), Mojave yucca (*Yucca schidigera*), and grasses such as big and little galleta (*Pleuraphis rigida* and *P. jamesii*) and side-oats gramma (*Bouteloua curtipendula*) are common in the eastern portions with summer rain. Other species found in the western Mojave, but not the eastern, include many winter annual herbs such as desert coreopsis

Blackbush (*Coleogyne ramosissima*) alliance
Death Valley National Park, Mojave Region
DFG photo: Todd Keeler-Wolf

(*Coreopsis bigelovii*), goldfields (*Lasthenia californica*), and California poppy (*Eschscholzia californica*). These and many other species present spectacular wildflower displays in good winter rainfall years.

Arrowweed (*Pluchea sericea*) alliance
Death Valley National Park, Mojave Region
DFG photo: Todd Keeler-Wolf

Alluvial fans and basins comprise much of the landscape of the Mojave Desert. Extensive alluvial fans form skirts around the mountains and fill much of the basins. They are typically vegetated with Creosote bush (*Larrea tridentata*)-burrobush (*Ambrosia dumosa*) scrub. The basins are vegetated with various salt-tolerant species. In some cases the basins are so salty that no vegetation occurs, and only remarkably flat playas and blinding white salt deposits exist.

More than a dozen dune systems occur in the Mojave. Many are occupied by unusual plant and animal species such as the Eureka dune grass (*Swallenia alexandrae*) and the Mojave fringe-toed lizard (*Uma scoparia*).

The higher desert mountains are topped with pinyon pine (*Pinus monophylla*) and, at the highest elevations, limber pine (*Pinus flexilis*) and bristlecone pine (*Pinus longaeva*). The mountains of the eastern Mojave contain much limestone and marble, and hold many limestone endemic plants.

Because the Mojave is so close to major metropolitan areas, such as the Los Angeles Basin, and includes several rapidly growing cities, the once wild and unpopulated Mojave is now compromised by the influences of civilization. In 1994, Congress enacted the California Desert Protection Act, designating large areas of the Mojave Desert as wilderness. Currently, the Bureau of Land Management and other cooperating agencies are working on management plans in an attempt to sustain the fascinating and fragile ecosystems of the Mojave Desert.

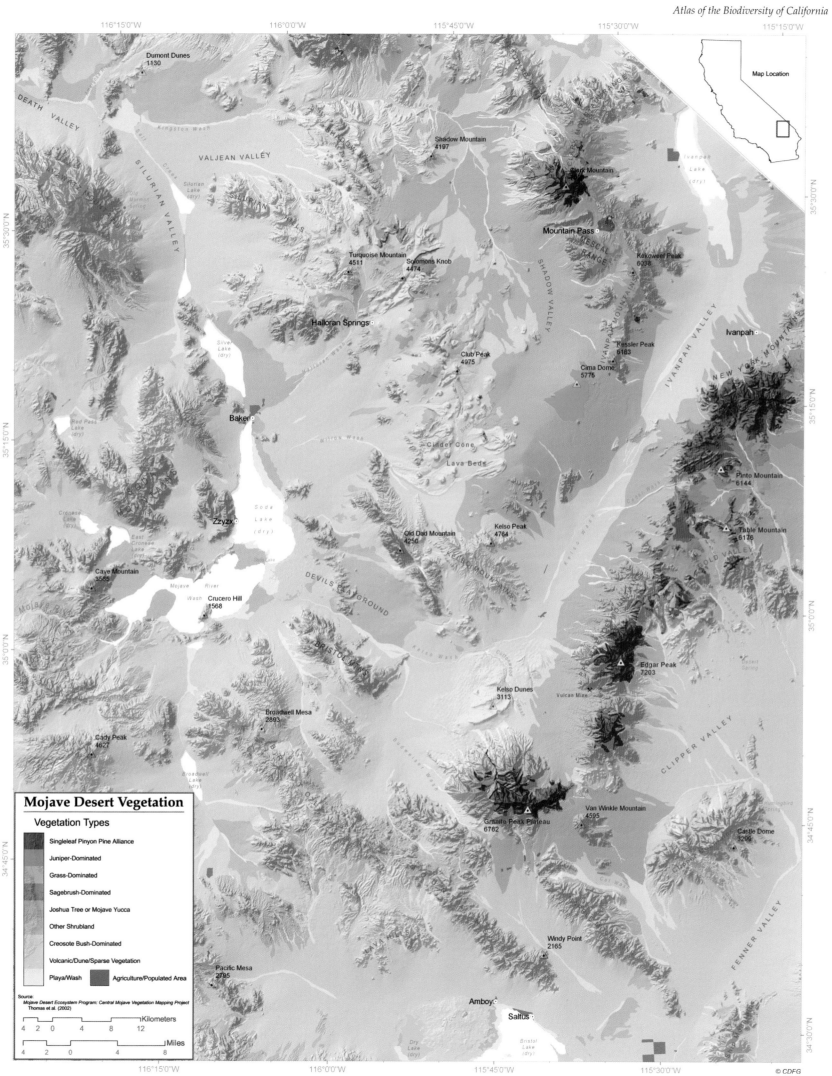

Map Location

DEATH VALLEY

Dumont Dunes
1130

Kingston Wash

VALJEAN VALLEY

Shadow Mountain
4197

Clark Mountain

SILURIAN VALLEY

Silurian Lake (dry)

Mountain Pass

MESCAL RANGE

SHADOW VALLEY

Kokoweef Peak
6038

Turquoise Mountain
4511

Solomons Knob
4474

Halloran Springs

Kessler Peak
6163

IVANPAH MOUNTAINS

IVANPAH VALLEY

Ivanpah

Silver Lake (dry)

Club Peak
4975

Cima Dome
5775

Baker

Halloran Wash

NEW YORK MOUNTAINS

Red Pass Lake (dry)

Wilson Wash

Cinder Cone

Lava Beds

Pinto Mountain
6144

Crenese Lake (dry)

Zzyzx

Soda Lake (dry)

Old Dad Mountain
4250

Kelso Peak
4764

Table Mountain
6176

East Cronese Lake (dry)

Cave Mountain
3565

Mojave River

Crucero Hill
1568

DEVILS PLAYGROUND

KELSO MOUNTAINS

Kelso Wash

Edgar Peak
7203

Desert Spring

BRISTOL MTNS

Kelso Wash

Vulcan Mine

Kelso Dunes
3113

Cady Peak
4627

Broadwell Mesa
2893

Van Winkle Mountain
4595

CLIPPER VALLEY

Broadwell Lake (dry)

Granite Peak Plateau
6762

Castle Dome
3299

LAVA HILLS

Pacific Mesa
2795

Windy Point
2165

FENNER VALLEY

Amboy

Saltus

Bristol Lake (dry)

Dry Lake (dry)

Mojave Desert Vegetation

Vegetation Types

- Singleleaf Pinyon Pine Alliance
- Juniper-Dominated
- Grass-Dominated
- Sagebrush-Dominated
- Joshua Tree or Mojave Yucca
- Other Shrubland
- Creosote Bush-Dominated
- Volcanic/Dune/Sparse Vegetation
- Playa/Wash
- Agriculture/Populated Area

Source:
Mojave Desert Ecosystem Program: Central Mojave Vegetation Mapping Project
Thomas et al. (2002)

Kilometers
4 2 0   4   8   12

Miles
4 2 0   4   8

© CDFG

Pupfishes of the Desert

By Becky Miller and Steve Parmenter

In California, pupfishes are good examples of native endemics with limited distribution. There are seven pupfish species or subspecies in the state. Four are generally restricted to a single spring with a limited outflow—Cottonball Marsh pupfish (*Cyprinodon salinus milleri*), Salt Creek pupfish (*C. s. salinus*), Saratoga Springs pupfish (*C. nevadensis nevadensis*), and Shoshone pupfish (*C. n. shoshone*). Three are limited to the remains of once much larger river and marsh systems—Owens pupfish (*C. radiosus*), Amargosa pupfish (*C. n. amargosae*), and desert pupfish (*C. macularius*). In some cases, successful reintroductions have extended the distribution of a pupfish taxon in California. With aquatic habitats so limited in the desert, it is not surprising that three of the seven are currently listed as threatened or endangered and that the rest are considered Species of Special Concern.

Desert pupfish (*Cyprinodon macularius*)
Photo © Dennis Flaherty

Pupfish are small (usually less than three inches from nose to tail), deep-bodied fish, with males slightly larger than females. They are often mistaken for minnows. However, unlike minnows, which have a toothless mouth, pupfish have a small mouth lined with teeth. Female pupfish are usually drab, olive-brown to brown, with from four to 10 vertical stripes. Non-breeding males look much like females. Breeding males, however, may exhibit bright blue or purple coloration. Some subspecies also have broad vertical bands on their sides or black bands on their tails. The breeding male desert pupfish exhibits a bright yellow-orange tail.

Desert pupfish habitat
San Felipe Creek, Colorado Desert Region
DFG photo: Darlene McGriff

Salt Creek pupfish
(*Cyprinodon salinus salinus*)
DFG photo: Phil Pister

The pressures of desert life demand a highly adapted fish. Pupfish have the ability to survive in incredibly harsh water conditions that would be lethal to most other fish species. Salinity in desert waters can be two to four times that of the ocean. The water temperature can vary from nearly freezing to 113 degrees Fahrenheit, and oxygen levels can be extremely low.

Pupfish are at a distinct disadvantage, however, in areas where they inhabit waters within the tolerance of introduced species. Because pupfish evolved in the absence of predatory fish, they do not possess the instinctive avoidance behavior necessary for survival in the presence of aggressive, aquatic species introduced by humans since the late 19th Century. When bass, mosquitofish, or crayfish, for example, are introduced into pupfish waters, the pupfish usually decline or disappear. This is due to competition or predation from the introduced species.

Salt Creek pupfish habitat
Salt Creek, Death Valley National Park, Mojave Region
DFG photo: Darlene McGriff

Another serious threat to the continued existence of the pupfish is the increasing human demand for water in the desert. Water pumped out of the ground depletes the same aquifers that supply water to the pupfish habitats. Desert cities require immense amounts of water. Well fields that supply water to a large city could potentially dry up springs and seeps many miles away.

Californians can help conserve pupfish by never moving wildlife from one place to another and by conserving water, especially in the desert.

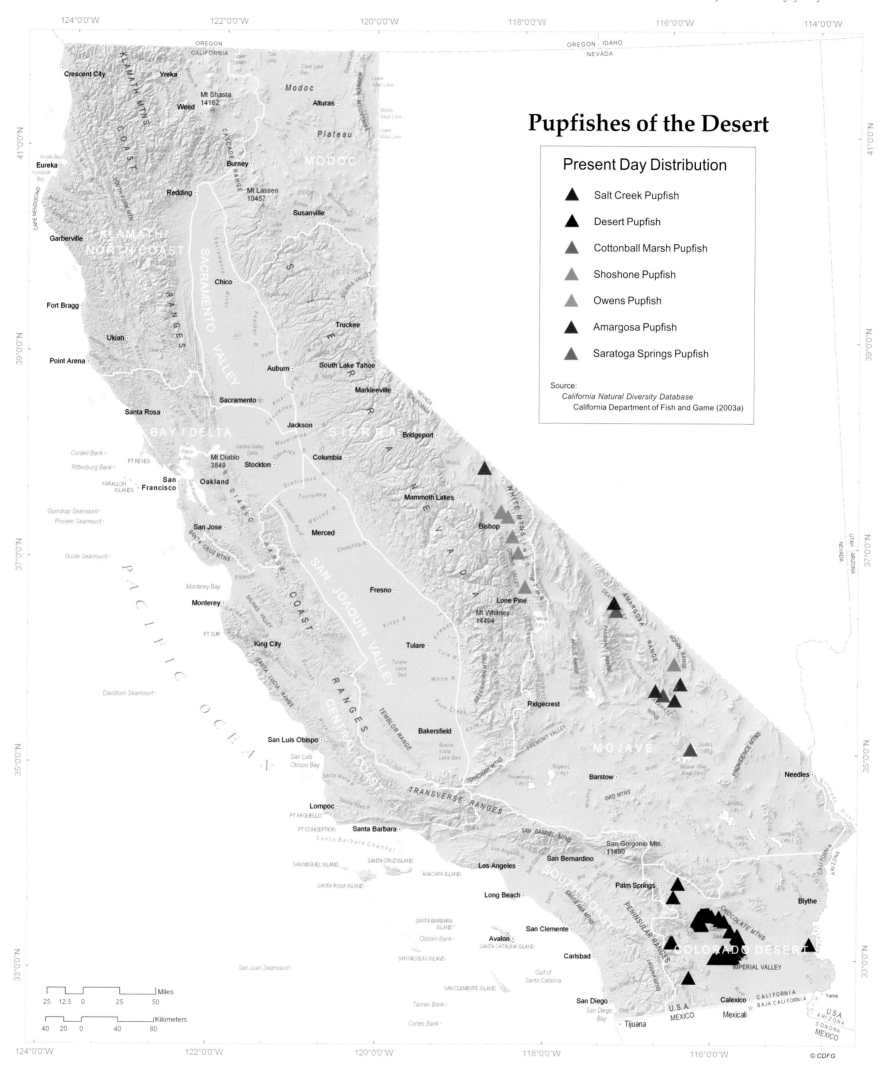

Pupfishes of the Desert

Present Day Distribution

▲ Salt Creek Pupfish

▲ Desert Pupfish

▲ Cottonball Marsh Pupfish

▲ Shoshone Pupfish

▲ Owens Pupfish

▲ Amargosa Pupfish

▲ Saratoga Springs Pupfish

Source:
California Natural Diversity Database
California Department of Fish and Game (2003a)

Pressures on Biodiversity

Gymnogyps californianus.

WINGSPAN: 9 feet

WEIGHT: 19.8 pounds

CALIFORNIA CONDOR

California's biodiversity faces many pressures. Most are tied to the effects of its human population, which is growing fastest in the Bay/Delta, Sacramento Valley, and South Coast regions. Threats to biodiversity in these regions are mostly due to the direct loss of habitat. However, the loss of continuous habitat is a pressure felt throughout the state as habitats are fragmented or migration corridors for wildlife are obstructed. A burgeoning population also places increasing demands on water and affects air and water quality. And, as human activity increases, so does the introduction of invasive plants and animals, an additional threat to native biodiversity.

Human Population

By Marc Hoshovsky and Eric Kauffman

Habitat loss due to human population growth presents the single greatest problem facing native plants and animals in California. The state's population will likely increase by approximately 11.3 million to just over 45 million people by the year 2020 (CDOF 2001). Most of this growth will concentrate in the South Coast, Central Valley, and San Francisco Bay areas. The counties of Los Angeles, Riverside, and San Bernardino combined will see an increase of 4.2 million people during this time period.

Human population growth creates new demands for housing, roads, jobs, schools, water, energy, and other infrastructure. Expansion of these services creates pressure to develop land at the expense of native habitat. This loss of habitat almost always results in native plants and animals being eliminated from the landscape.

Recent trends and future predictions indicate that existing urban areas will see the largest population increases in California during the next 40 years. Such increases in existing cities generally do not result in great losses of additional natural habitat acreage, because they are absorbed through infill projects or increases along the edges, and because the required large scale infrastructure is usually already in place. However, local endemic species may be greatly affected as their remaining habitat areas are developed or subjected to an increasing human presence.

It is the rapid population growth in California's more rural areas—the Central Valley, Sierra Nevada foothills, and the Southern California Coast Ranges—that presents a more troubling trend for native plants and animals. While not matching the growth predictions for the San Francisco Bay Area or South Coast, population growth in these areas is still predicted to be very high. These areas are likely to have housing densities much lower than in the major cities. The combination of high population growth in rural areas and expected low housing densities means that substantially more land presently in natural habitat will be converted to housing. Urban expansion into rural areas compounds the problem because these

areas generally lack the infrastructure to handle new growth. Consequently, new residential and industrial development requires transportation, water, sewer, and other services to be greatly expanded or newly built, only aggravating the cost to habitat.

The expected impact of this growth on species and habitats is currently being analyzed by state resource agencies. Unless altered, such a continued rate of habitat consumption by urban growth will lead to substantial losses in biodiversity in the future.

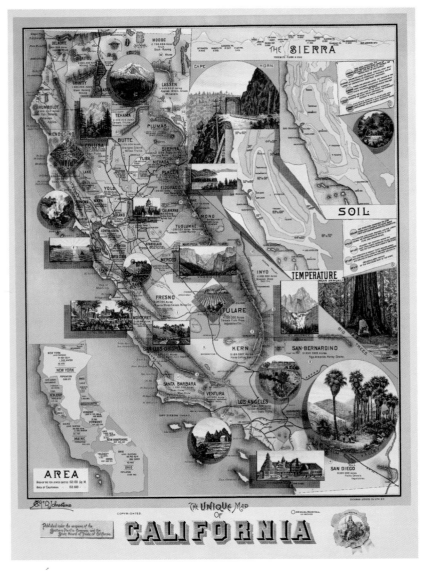

This "Unique Map of California," published in 1888 by the Southern Pacific Railroad Company and the State Board of Trade, was meant to attract people and business to the state by extolling the diversity of California's natural resources, topography, climate, soils, and agriculture.
Source: Library of Congress, Geography and Map Division

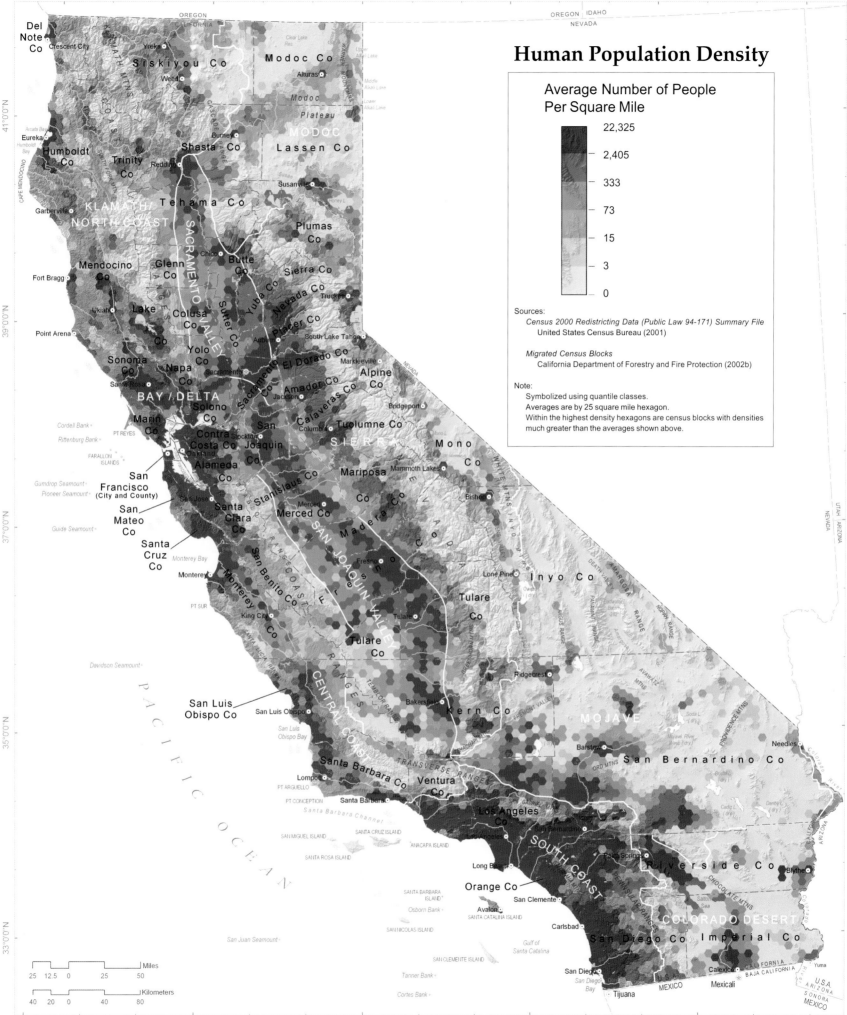

Human Population Density

Average Number of People
Per Square Mile

22,325

2,405

333

73

15

3

0

Sources:
Census 2000 Redistricting Data (Public Law 94-171) Summary File
United States Census Bureau (2001)

Migrated Census Blocks
California Department of Forestry and Fire Protection (2002b)

Note:
Symbolized using quantile classes.
Averages are by 25 square mile hexagon.
Within the highest density hexagons are census blocks with densities
much greater than the averages shown above.

© CDFG

Introduced Invasive Plants: Yellow Starthistle

By Diana Hickson

Since the arrival of Europeans, approximately 1,000 plant species from many parts of the globe have become established in the state's wildlands. Some of these species have the ability to spread aggressively into native ecosystems, displacing native plants and the wildlife species that depend on them. The California Exotic Pest Plant Council lists about 140 such species on their list of Plants of Greatest Ecological Concern, including such weeds as giant reed (*Arundo donax*), European beachgrass (*Ammophila arenaria*), Scotch broom (*Cytisus scoparius*), and yellow starthistle (*Centaurea solstitialis*).

Giant reed (*Arundo donax*) invading riparian habitat. Photo © Roxanne Bittman

Introduced invasive plants affect native biodiversity in several ways. They may displace native plant species, or they may change the way a normal ecosystem operates. Tamarisk (*Tamarix* spp.), for example, is an aggressive invader of desert riparian habitats, where it can form impenetrable thickets that suck up water so that other plants, birds, and even the endangered desert pupfish (*Cyprinodon macularius*) are left high and dry.

Invasive weeds not only affect biodiversity but have recreational, aesthetic, and economic impacts. For example, water hyacinth (*Eichhornia crassipes*), an escaped ornamental aquatic plant in the Sacramento-San Joaquin Delta, clogs boating

Jubata grass (*Cortaderia jubata*) invading coniferous forest. Photo © Joseph Carboni

waterways, while jubata grass (*Cortaderia jubata*), a forestry pest, outcompetes seedling pine trees in logged forests.

Yellow starthistle (*Centaurea solstitialis*) DFG photo: Roxanne Bittman

Yellow starthistle is the most widespread weed of wildlands of the state. Native to Eurasia, it was first found in Alameda County in 1869, and has since spread to 55 of the state's 58 counties, infesting up to 42 percent of California (Pitcairn et al. 1998).

Yellow starthistle displaces native plant species, decreases range forage quality, and can be lethal to horses if consumed in sufficient amounts. Its spiny flowerheads are a bane to hikers and other outdoor enthusiasts.

Yellow starthistle (*Centaurea solstitialis*) DFG photo: Roxanne Bittman

Management of this weed can include several techniques, such as timed intensive cattle grazing, mowing, burning, and restoring an area with native plant species (DiTomaso et al. 2000). Additionally, the Agricultural Research Service of the United States Department of Agriculture and the California Department of Food and Agriculture (CDFA) have introduced biological control agents (natural insect pests of the plant) in an attempt to reduce yellow starthistle abundance.

The map at right is from CDFA's yellow starthistle mapping project, which uses a legal township (36 square miles) for a sample area. For each township, three levels of infestation—none, low, or high—are recorded.

Introduced Invasive Plants: Yellow Starthistle

Starthistle Infestation by Township

High

Low

Source:
Starthistle Infestation by Township.
California Department of Food and Agriculture (1997)

© CDFG

Introduced Invasive Animals: Imported Red Fox

By Ron Jurek

For over two centuries, people have imported animals that are not native to California. Whether brought here intentionally for food, sport, ornament, or pet uses, or by accident, many of them have now been introduced in the wild, to the detriment of California's natural environment.

Red foxes (*Vulpes vulpes*) from the central or eastern United States were imported into the Sacramento Valley as early as the 1870s, perhaps for hunting, rodent control, or nostalgic reasons. When the Transcontinental Railroad was completed in 1869, cross-country rail trips took only days, allowing importation of foxes and other animals that would not have survived long voyages by ship or wagon. In the 1920s, when fur farming began, other varieties of red foxes were imported. Even after animal importation restrictions were enacted in 1933, red foxes were imported for pets, exhibition, and other reasons. Undoubtedly, many escaped or were released.

In the 1970s, introduced foxes were still found mainly in the Sacramento Valley. Only a decade later, red foxes were appearing widely from the San Francisco and Sacramento areas to Southern California, becoming a serious threat to wildlife. This rapid expansion may

Imported red fox (*Vulpes vulpes*) with ground squirrel
Photo © Don Moore

have been aided by well-meaning people who, in recent decades, relocated nuisance or rehabilitated foxes long distances. In an hour by vehicle, introduced animals advance dozens of miles, far surpassing natural movements. In 1988, two introduced red foxes were illegally relocated 200 miles into the range of the Sierra Nevada red fox (*V. v. necator*), a threatened subspecies endemic to the high Sierra and Cascade ranges. It is not known if the two foxes survived, but their release potentially increased threats to the native population through competition, predation, hybridization, and the spread of disease.

Red fox predation and disturbance are disastrous for native wildlife. Populations of threatened or endangered Clapper Rail (*Rallus longirostris*), Least Tern (*Sterna antillarum*), and Snowy Plover (*Charadrius alexandrinus*) inhabiting our coastal marshes and beaches were depleted by these newcomers in the 1980s, before control efforts began. Red foxes are still a threat in many areas. These foxes are highly adaptable and survive well in urban areas. Some wildlife reserves are too small to support native coyotes (*Canis latrans*) and, in the absence of these larger predators, red foxes can invade and thrive.

Introduced red foxes probably cannot be eliminated from California, but in local habitats with vulnerable native species, fox control efforts are necessary and effective.

Imported red fox (*Vulpes vulpes*)
Photo © Don Moore

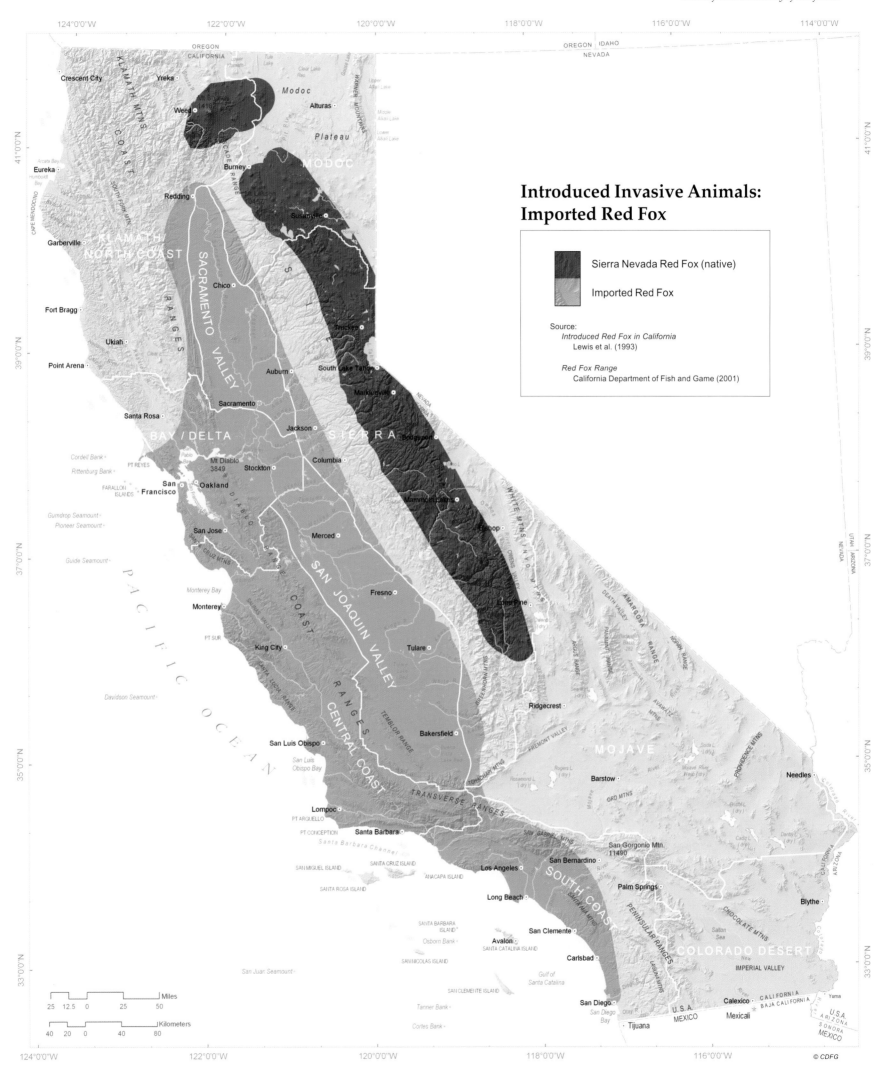

**Introduced Invasive Animals:
Imported Red Fox**

Sierra Nevada Red Fox (native)

Imported Red Fox

Source:
Introduced Red Fox in California
Lewis et al. (1993)

Red Fox Range
California Department of Fish and Game (2001)

© CDFG

Introduced Invasive Animals: Chinese Mitten Crab

By Kathy Hieb

The Chinese mitten crab (*Eriocheir sinensis*) is one of the more recent of California's many aquatic invaders. It is native to coastal rivers and estuaries in China and Korea, and is a highly prized delicacy in Asia. In California, the first mitten crabs were observed in South San Francisco Bay in 1992. They spread rapidly throughout the San Francisco Estuary and much of the Central Valley. In the fall of 1998, mitten crabs were found from Colusa and Yuba counties in the north to Merced County in the south. They were also found in Cirby Creek in Placer County and other Sierra Nevada foothill streams. In 1999 and 2000, the numbers and distribution of the crab decreased from 1998. Although we do not understand what factors control the crab's population, we expect their numbers to cycle up and down.

to the bottom in late spring and migrate upstream to brackish and then fresh water over several months. They remain in fresh water for one to two years, with some crabs migrating even further upstream their second year. In the fall of their second or third year, they migrate back to salt water to complete the life cycle. Juvenile mitten crabs eat mostly plant material, but adult crabs consume a variety of items, including clams, worms, and shrimp.

Where it occurs in large numbers, the mitten crab has caused several problems—damaging catch in commercial fishing nets, clogging small pumps and water systems at power plants, hindering fish salvage efforts at state and federal

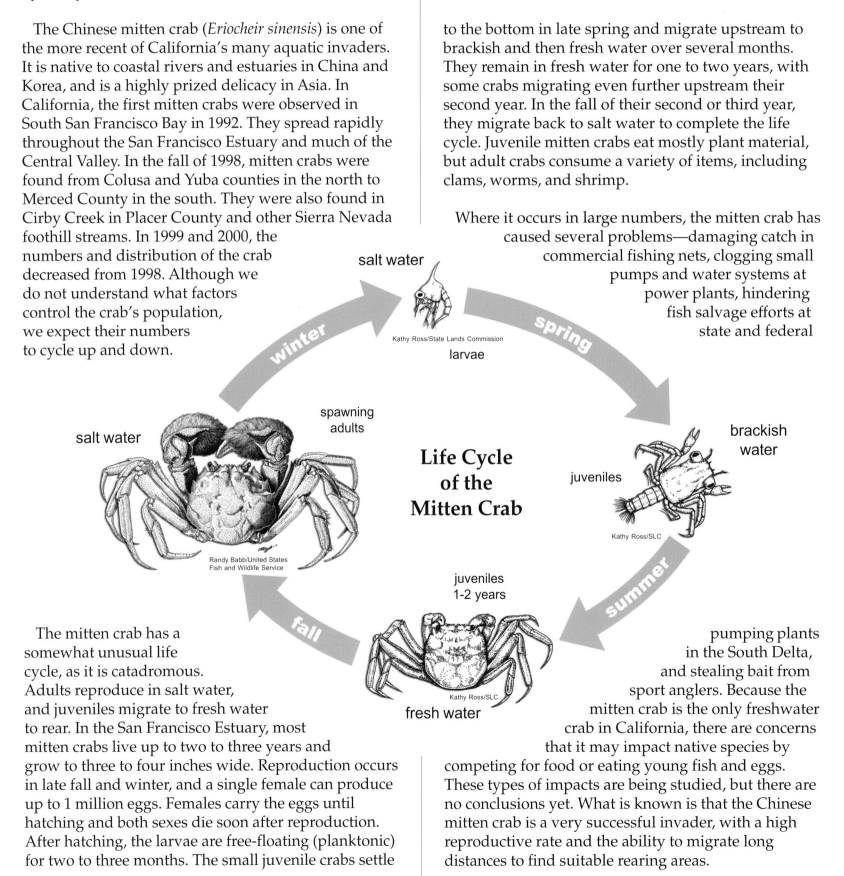

salt water

Kathy Ross/State Lands Commission

larvae

winter

spring

Life Cycle of the Mitten Crab

spawning adults

salt water

Randy Babb/United States Fish and Wildlife Service

juveniles

brackish water

Kathy Ross/SLC

summer

juveniles 1-2 years

fall

fresh water

Kathy Ross/SLC

The mitten crab has a somewhat unusual life cycle, as it is catadromous. Adults reproduce in salt water, and juveniles migrate to fresh water to rear. In the San Francisco Estuary, most mitten crabs live up to two to three years and grow to three to four inches wide. Reproduction occurs in late fall and winter, and a single female can produce up to 1 million eggs. Females carry the eggs until hatching and both sexes die soon after reproduction. After hatching, the larvae are free-floating (planktonic) for two to three months. The small juvenile crabs settle

pumping plants in the South Delta, and stealing bait from sport anglers. Because the mitten crab is the only freshwater crab in California, there are concerns that it may impact native species by competing for food or eating young fish and eggs. These types of impacts are being studied, but there are no conclusions yet. What is known is that the Chinese mitten crab is a very successful invader, with a high reproductive rate and the ability to migrate long distances to find suitable rearing areas.

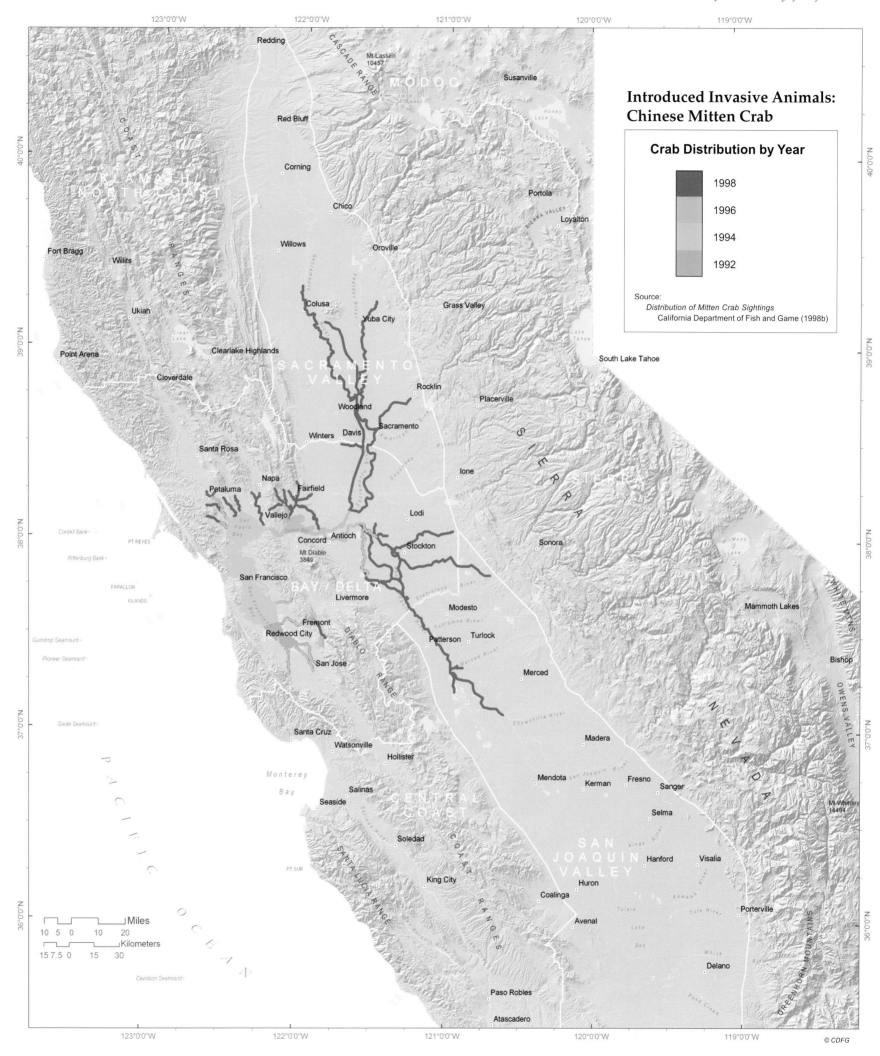

Introduced Invasive Animals:
Chinese Mitten Crab

Crab Distribution by Year

1998
1996
1994
1992

Source:
Distribution of Mitten Crab Sightings
California Department of Fish and Game (1998b)

Sustaining Biodiversity

Ardea alba.

GREAT EGRET

Public and private efforts to sustain California's biodiversity are occurring throughout the state. Strategies for sustaining biodiversity at a statewide or regional level include land ownership or management, conservation planning, and environmental law. Virtually all strategies are coordinated efforts between government agencies, organizations, and individuals with a common interest in conserving the biodiversity of California.

Department of Fish and Game Lands

By Ronald Rempel

The Department of Fish and Game, in cooperation with its partners, manages over 932,000 acres of wildlife habitat in California, and owns about 488,000 of these acres. Lands are acquired on behalf of the Department by the Wildlife Conservation Board and are designated as Wildlife Areas or Ecological Reserves by the Fish and Game Commission.

These lands are managed to preserve the biological diversity of the state. However, the management focus of different parcels may vary greatly depending on the purposes for which each parcel was acquired, the management plan for the property, and the recreational opportunities it can provide.

There are 108 state Wildlife Areas encompassing almost 650,000 acres. Wildlife Areas are typically lands that are managed for both biological diversity and significant populations of waterfowl, upland game birds (such as quail, turkey, or pheasant), deer, elk, and other common species. They also provide opportunities for fishing, hunting, wildlife viewing, and other wildlife dependent recreational activities.

The 121 state Ecological Reserves, encompassing approximately 130,000 acres, are managed to preserve

Bonnie Doon Ecological Reserve,
Central Coast Region
Photo © Caitlin Bean

the state's biological diversity, special status species, unique habitats, and critical portions of natural communities. Although Ecological Reserves are primarily established to conserve their ecological values, activities including scientific research, outdoor education, wildlife viewing, hiking, or limited hunting and fishing may be permitted on some of them.

The Department of Fish and Game also manages nearly 74,000 acres of conservation easements. Conservation easements protect land from conversion to other uses, including development, while allowing fee title ownership to rest with private individuals, corporations, non-profit groups, or public agencies other than the Department. This mechanism is often used to promote cooperation between agencies, local communities, and conservation organizations while still protecting valuable wildlife resources. A wide variety of species and habitats are protected through conservation easements including wetlands, riparian habitat, vernal pools, coastal sage scrub, old growth forest, native grasslands, and deer habitat.

In combination with lands managed by other state, federal, and local agencies, conservation groups, land trusts, and private individuals, Department lands are the foundation securing the long term protection of California's biological diversity. While this foundation has been laid, much more land will have to be conserved to ensure the permanent protection of the biodiversity of the state.

DFG Administered Lands by Primary Purpose and Designation

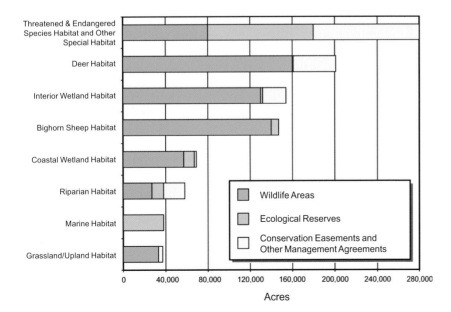

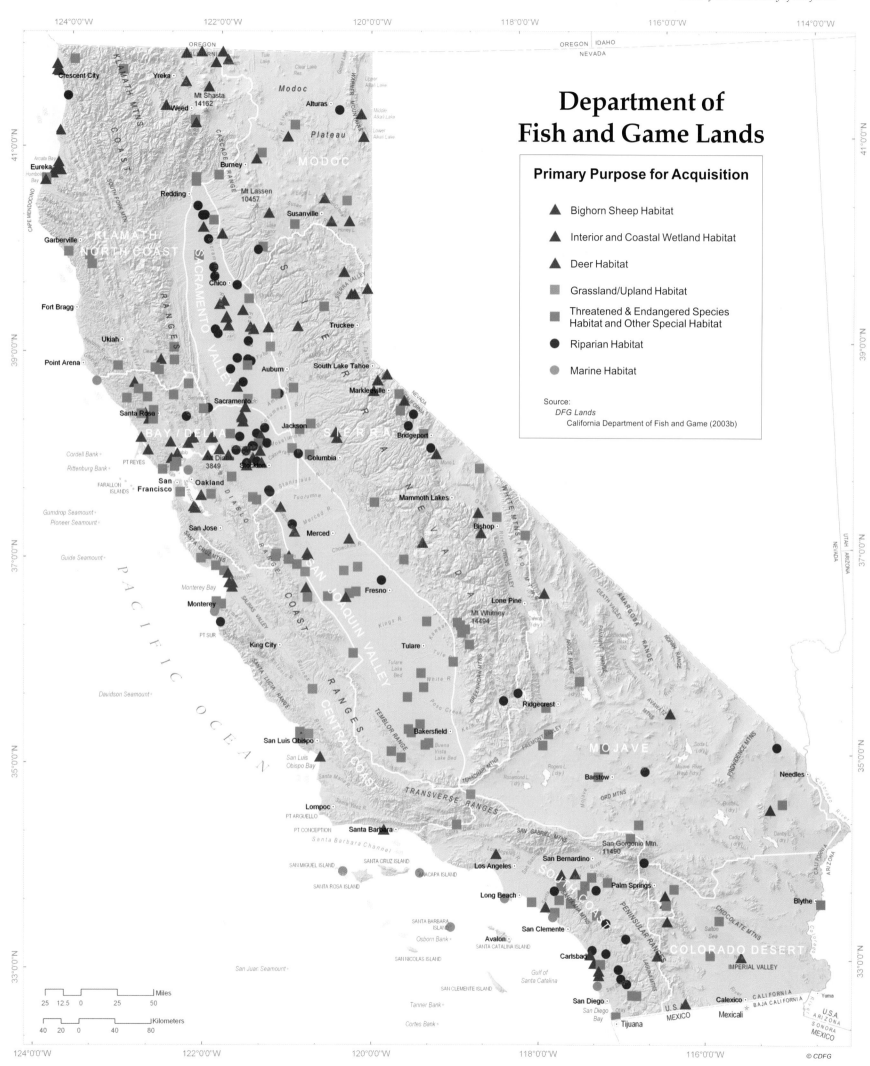

Department of Fish and Game Lands

Primary Purpose for Acquisition

▲ Bighorn Sheep Habitat

▲ Interior and Coastal Wetland Habitat

▲ Deer Habitat

■ Grassland/Upland Habitat

■ Threatened & Endangered Species Habitat and Other Special Habitat

● Riparian Habitat

● Marine Habitat

Source:
DFG Lands
California Department of Fish and Game (2003b)

© CDFG

Regional Conservation Planning

By Gail Presley

California's human population is expected to increase by 33 percent by the year 2020, to almost 46 million people. Due to widespread land conversion that will be required to support human needs, many species and natural communities are at risk of being lost. The heaviest growth is projected to occur in central and Southern California, in areas that comprise several national biodiversity "hotspots" (page 3).

Conservation biologists have determined that the most effective way to ensure survival of species is to protect natural areas large enough to maintain the diversity of habitats, species, and processes that occur there. People also recognize that having wildlands surrounding their neighborhoods and cities is an important aspect of their quality of life.

To address the conflicts between population growth and preservation of California's rich biological diversity, the Department of Fish and Game developed the Natural Community Conservation Planning (NCCP) program. The NCCP program relies on cooperation among government agencies at local, state, and federal levels; business and industry groups; landowners (more than 50 percent of special status species occur on private land); conservation organizations; and the public. NCCP plans integrate the principles of conservation biology, state and federal endangered species laws, and local land use planning. The map at right shows the locations of both NCCP and Habitat Conservation Planning (HCP) areas. HCPs provide for the protection of specific endangered

Residential development in coastal sage scrub, South Coast Region
DFG photo: Betsy Bolster

species in cooperation with the United States Fish and Wildlife Service in a process complementary to NCCP.

Besides facilitating the NCCP process, the Department has contributed toward the creation of regional preserves by acquiring habitat through the Wildlife Conservation Board. For example, the Board has purchased more than 17,000 acres of land supporting special status species and sensitive habitats for Southern California NCCP preserves, including coastal sage scrub, sand dunes, vernal pools, and riparian areas. The Department, Fish and Wildlife Service, local governments, and non-profit organizations are working together as partners to manage and monitor these lands for the benefit of special status species.

The Department has an annual grant program available to local governments, academic institutions, and non-profit groups to help fund conservation tasks for approved plans. It has awarded grants to assess the biological resources of preserves, monitor special status species and sensitive habitats, map vegetation, manage data using geographic information systems, and restore habitat on preserve lands.

Long term monitoring and management will continue to guide the NCCP and HCP processes as new regional efforts are initiated throughout the state. The Department encourages partnerships to form landscape-level strategies for wildlife and habitat conservation. It is a reliable method to address the pressures from economic and human population growth in California.

The impending federal listing of California Gnatcatcher (*Polioptila californica*) as a threatened species was a primary impetus for the creation of the NCCP program in 1991. This species inhabits coastal sage scrub.
Photo © James Gallagher

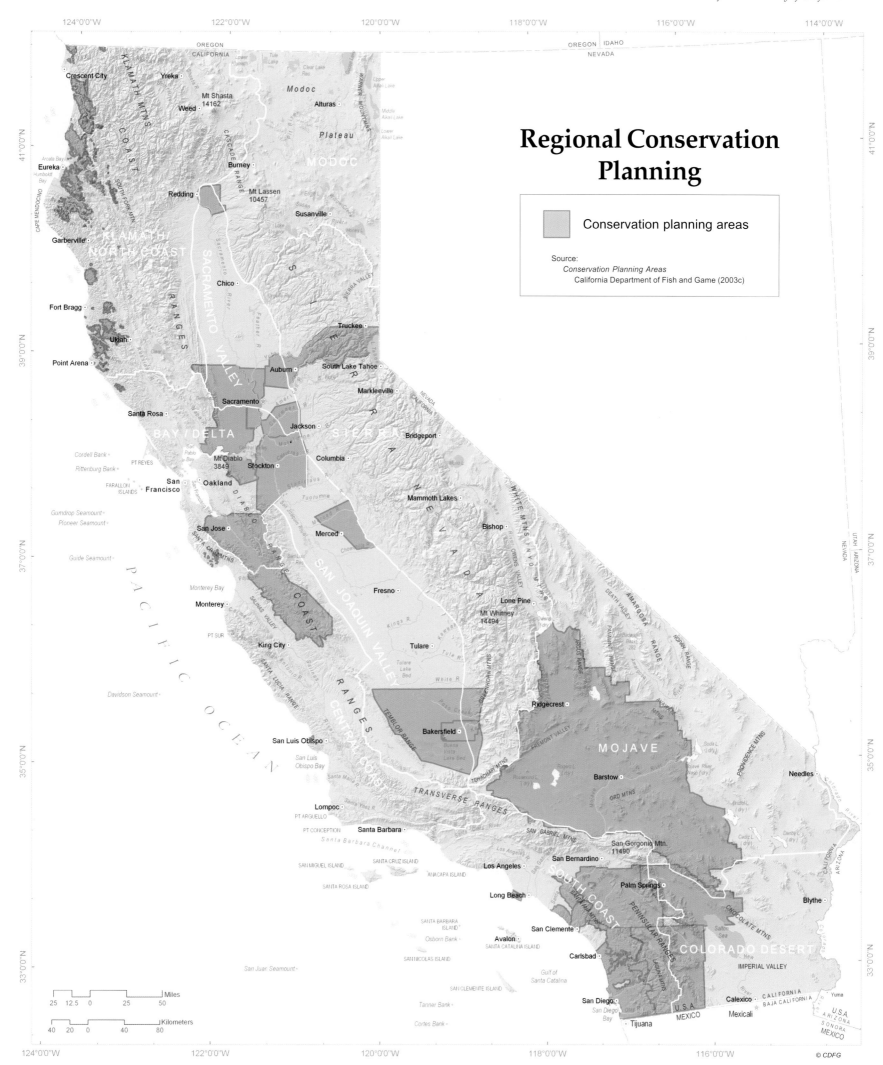

Regional Conservation Planning

Conservation planning areas

Source:
Conservation Planning Areas
California Department of Fish and Game (2003c)

© CDFG

Joint Ventures

By Diana Hickson

Bird conservation is the focus of six Joint Ventures working in California. These Joint Ventures are cooperative partnerships between federal, state, and local governments, businesses, conservation organizations, and individual citizens. Several of these Joint Ventures are components of the North American Waterfowl Management Plan, an effort by Canada, the United States, and Mexico to restore waterfowl and other migratory bird populations by protecting and restoring wetland habitat from the Canadian Arctic to the Gulf of Mexico. Other Joint Ventures were created as components of Partners in Flight, a national movement to protect and restore viable populations of North American non-game land birds. Despite their different origins, all Joint Ventures help to conserve not only birds but other species as well, including reptiles, fishes, mammals, invertebrates, and plants.

The Central Valley Habitat Joint Venture (CVHJV) works to protect and restore wetlands in California's Central Valley, which is critically important to wintering waterfowl in the Pacific Flyway, supporting 60 percent of the total duck and goose population. At one time, the Central Valley included an estimated 4 million acres of wetlands. By 2000, this number had dwindled to 170,000, a 96 percent loss due mainly to wetland conversion by agriculture, flood control, navigation projects, and urban expansion. Approximately 30 percent of the wetlands that still exist are located within national wildlife refuges and state wildlife areas. The remaining 70 percent are privately owned and managed primarily as duck hunting clubs.

Voting members of the CVHJV management board include the California Waterfowl Association, Ducks Unlimited, National Audubon Society, The Nature Conservancy, Point Reyes Bird Observatory, The Trust for Public Land, and American Farmland Trust. Non-voting state agencies represented include the Department of Fish and Game, Wildlife Conservation Board, and Department of Water Resources. Federal agencies include the Fish and Wildlife Service, Bureau of Reclamation, Environmental Protection Agency, Corps of Engineers, Natural Resources Conservation Service, and Bureau of Land Management.

Yellow-breasted Chat (*Icteria virens*) is one of the 14 riparian-associated bird species selected by the Riparian Habitat Joint Venture to serve as indicators of the condition of natural riparian habitat.
Photo © Bob Corey

Since the program's inception, the CVHJV partners have combined to protect or restore more than 130,000 acres of wetlands within the Central Valley. In 1990, the Inland Wetlands Conservation Program was established within the Wildlife Conservation Board with the sole purpose of carrying out the programs of the CVHJV. In addition, all of the partners have benefited from cost sharing funds such as those provided by the North American Wetlands Conservation Act.

Five other Joint Ventures are working in California. The Riparian Habitat Joint Venture (RHJV) seeks to facilitate a statewide, coordinated effort to restore and protect riparian habitat, which now covers less than five percent of its historical range but is perhaps the most important habitat for land bird species in the state. The RHJV has developed the Riparian Bird Conservation Plan, which identifies 14 birds as focal species. An Implementation Strategy is now being drafted for their conservation. The San Francisco Bay Joint Venture focuses on the nation's second largest and perhaps the most biologically significant estuary on the Pacific Coast. It has plans to protect, enhance, or restore over 200,000 acres of lagoons, seasonal wetlands, and tidal flats and marshes over the next 20 years. The Sonoran Joint Venture works to conserve habitat for the more than 500 bird species that breed or winter in, or migrate through the Sonoran Desert, a biologically and culturally rich area in northwest Mexico, Arizona, and the southeast corner of California. The Intermountain West Joint Venture covers portions of 12 western states, with a goal of restoring and enhancing 1 million acres of wetland habitat. Almost two thirds of this habitat are on state or federal lands, though the key to success will be securing adequate water supply to support the wetlands. The Pacific Coast Joint Venture area includes coastal Alaska, British Columbia, Washington, all of western Oregon, and coastal Northern California, focusing on the protection of coastal wetland habitat.

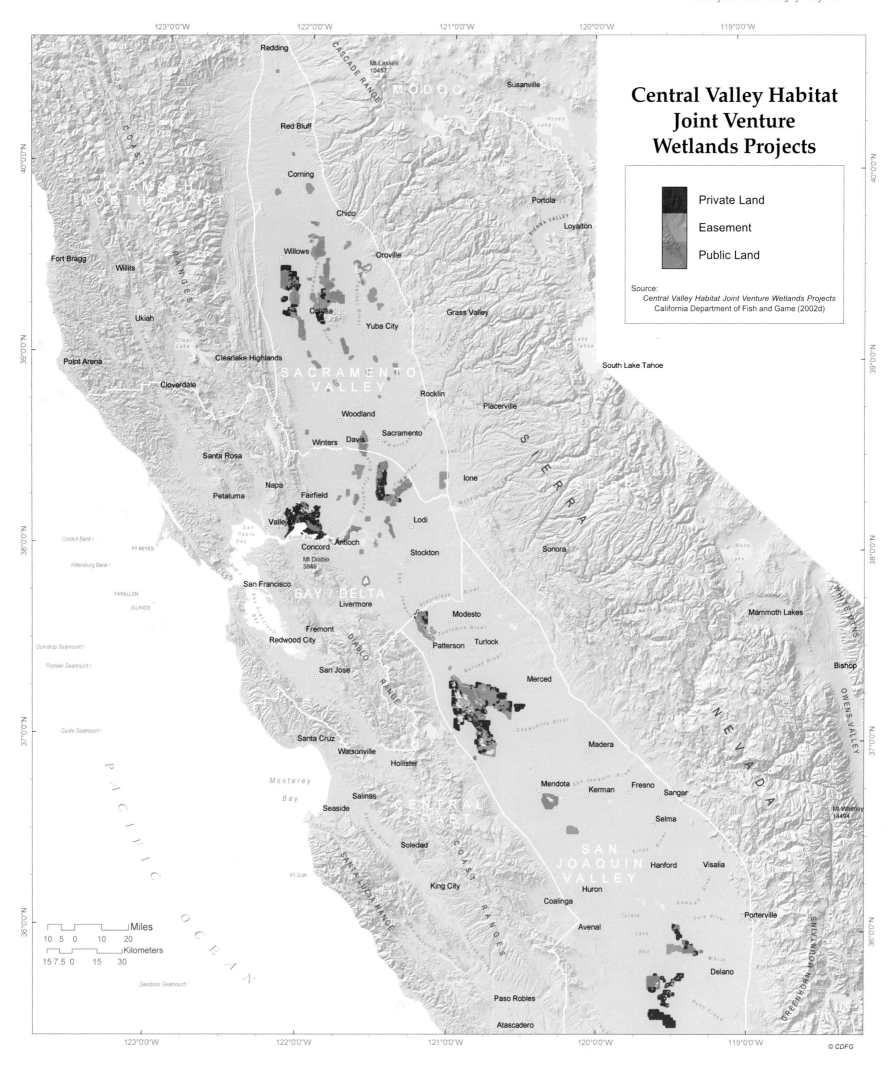

Central Valley Habitat
Joint Venture
Wetlands Projects

Private Land

Easement

Public Land

Source:
Central Valley Habitat Joint Venture Wetlands Projects
California Department of Fish and Game (2002d)

CALFED Bay-Delta Program

By Diana Jacobs

The San Francisco Bay–Sacramento and San Joaquin Delta system is the largest estuary on the United States Pacific Coast. The brackish and freshwater components of the estuary, commonly referred to as "the Delta," comprise a rich and complex system of wetland and aquatic habitats formed at the confluence of two major river systems. The Delta and its watershed have been drastically altered by human activity, starting with the California Gold Rush in 1849-1850. Marsh reclamation, agriculture, urbanization, introduction of invasive species, and large water supply and flood control public works projects followed.

Many species depend on the Delta, particularly native fishes such as salmon (*Oncorhynchus* spp.), steelhead (*O. mykiss irideus*), and delta smelt (*Hypomesus transpacificus*). Populations of these species have shown severe declines.

Delta smelt
(*Hypomesus transpacificus*)
Photo © B. Moose Peterson

The present-day Delta is also the physical hub of California's two largest water distribution systems, supplying drinking water to two thirds of the state's population and irrigation water for over 7 million acres of farmland. Conflicts between ecosystem and human needs have resulted in a daunting problem of engineering and environmental management.

In 1995, the California and federal governments joined together to form the CALFED Bay-Delta Program. CALFED is a consortium of the major agencies with principle authority over fish and wildlife and water resources in the Delta and its watershed.

Sacramento – San Joaquin Delta, Bay/Delta Region
Photo © Department of Water Resources

The CALFED agencies, working with stakeholders, have crafted a 30 year plan to improve the quality and reliability of the state's water supplies and to restore the ecological health of the Bay-Delta and its watershed. Adopted in 2000, the plan contains 11 program elements, including the Ecosystem Restoration Program (ERP). The ERP works to sustain biodiversity in the Bay-Delta and its watershed and has already funded almost 400 restoration projects totaling about $400 million. These projects represent a variety of strategies for ecological restoration, including habitat protection, fish passage improvements, invasive species management, water quality enhancement, and scientific research. In the fall of 2002, the governor signed into law the California Bay-Delta Authority Act, which creates a new authority within the California Resources Agency to coordinate and oversee implementation of the CALFED program.

Clapper Rail
(*Rallus longirostris*),
Hill Slough, Suisun Marsh,
Bay/Delta Region
Photo © Brenda Grewell

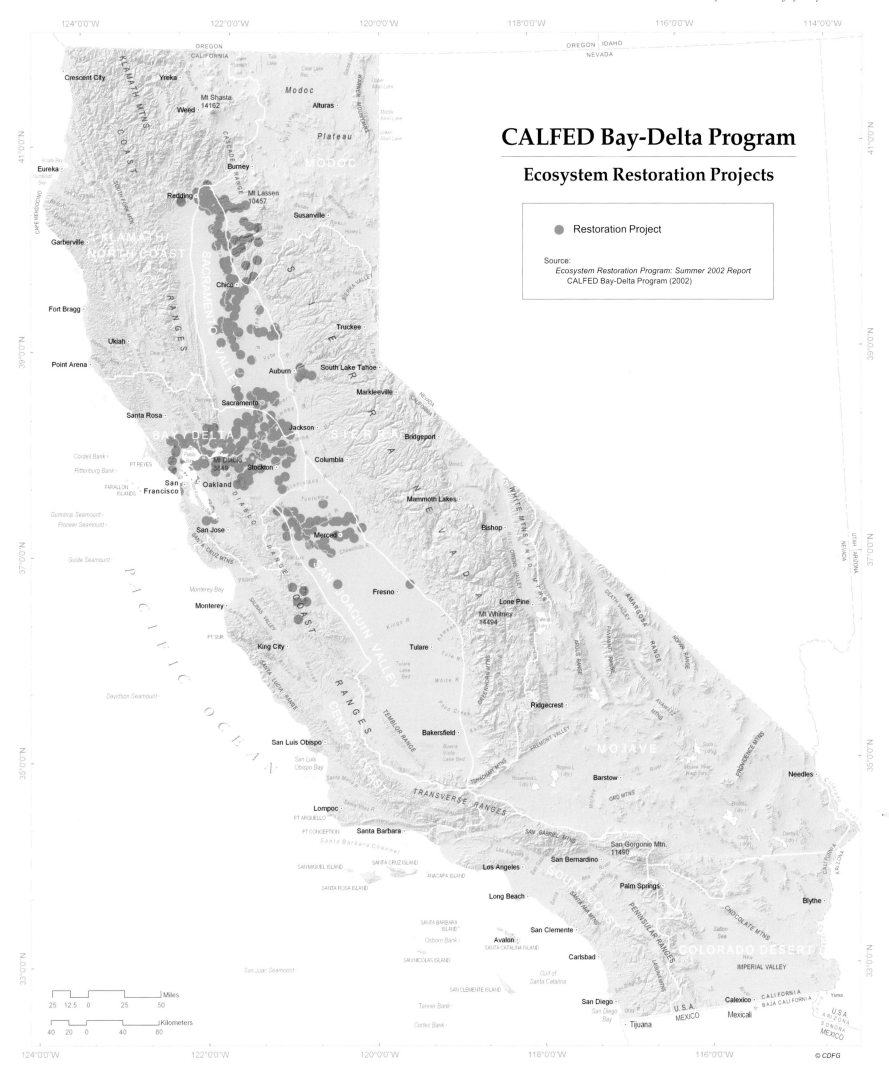

CALFED Bay-Delta Program

Ecosystem Restoration Projects

● Restoration Project

Source:
Ecosystem Restoration Program: Summer 2002 Report
CALFED Bay-Delta Program (2002)

© CDFG

Coastal Fisheries Restoration Grants

By Helen Birss

The Fisheries Restoration Grant Program is a collaborative effort that focuses on restoring anadromous fish habitat to ensure the survival and protection of salmon and steelhead trout in coastal areas of California. The program was established in 1981 in response to rapidly declining populations of salmon and steelhead trout and deteriorating salmonid habitat in California. The Department of Fish and Game manages the program, which is funded with state and federal resources, and also relies on partnerships with contributing local governments, tribes, water districts, fisheries organizations, watershed restoration groups, the California Conservation Corps, AmeriCorps, and private landowners.

South Fork Eel River,
Klamath/North Coast Region
Photo © Marc Hoshovsky

This competitive grant program has invested over $100 million and supports a variety of projects from sediment reduction to watershed education throughout coastal California. The majority of these funds are awarded for habitat restoration projects that improve overhead cover, spawning gravels, and pool habitat; reduce or eliminate erosion and sedimentation impacts; screen sites where water is diverted for agricultural and urban uses so fish remain in their habitat; and remove barriers to fish passage along streams and rivers.

Funds have also been awarded for activities that indirectly affect habitat restoration. Examples are cooperative fish rearing, acquisition of riparian easements, project monitoring, watershed assessment and planning, support for watershed organizations, and public outreach.

Outreach projects have included classroom education for children, as well as technical workshops for adults and watershed groups involved in restoration projects. The result has been an increased awareness about the habitat conditions necessary for anadromous fish to thrive. The program has also exposed thousands of young people to the importance of maintaining the integrity of our watersheds.

Restoring anadromous salmon and steelhead habitat is a commitment that this program and its partners have embraced in order to maintain and restore California's diverse ecosystems for generations to come. With population levels of some salmon at critically low levels, there are many opportunities for restoration projects that will benefit salmon and steelhead trout in California.

The map at right shows the location of stream restoration projects.

The map below shows the location of outreach and planning projects designed to foster community involvement and promote future restoration efforts.

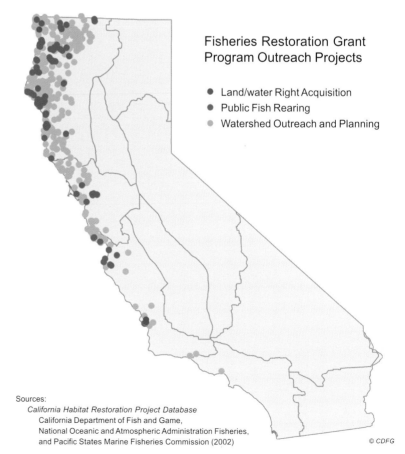

Fisheries Restoration Grant Program Outreach Projects

- Land/water Right Acquisition
- Public Fish Rearing
- Watershed Outreach and Planning

Sources:
California Habitat Restoration Project Database
California Department of Fish and Game,
National Oceanic and Atmospheric Administration Fisheries,
and Pacific States Marine Fisheries Commission (2002)

© CDFG

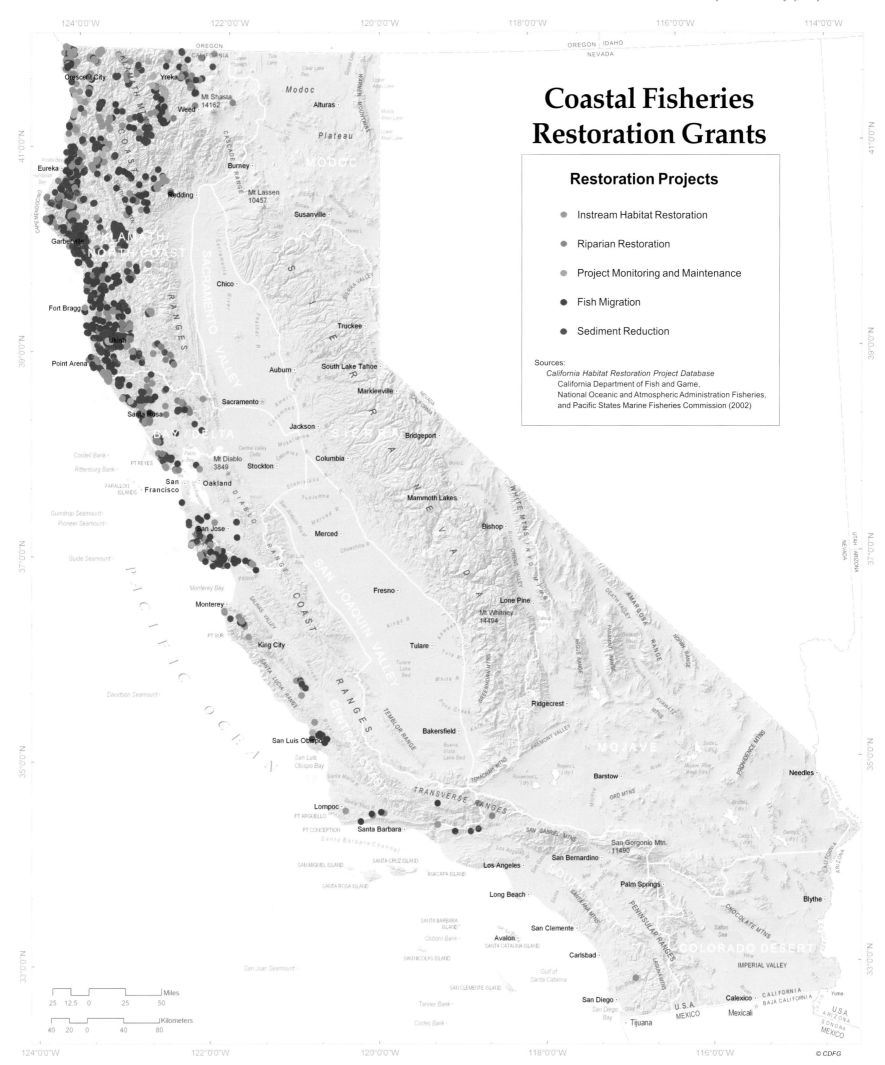

Coastal Fisheries Restoration Grants

Restoration Projects

- Instream Habitat Restoration
- Riparian Restoration
- Project Monitoring and Maintenance
- Fish Migration
- Sediment Reduction

Sources:
California Habitat Restoration Project Database
California Department of Fish and Game,
National Oceanic and Atmospheric Administration Fisheries,
and Pacific States Marine Fisheries Commission (2002)

© CDFG

Glossary

alluvial fan — a wide, cone-shaped deposit of rocks, sand, gravel, and finer materials that has been deposited by a stream as it flows out of a mountainous area onto a plain.

alluvium — river or stream deposits, such as sand and silt.

anadromous — refers to fish **species** that spend most of their lives in the ocean but **migrate** to freshwater rivers and streams to spawn.

aquatic — growing, living in, or frequenting water, usually open water; compare with **wetland**.

aquifer — an underground reservoir of water.

batholith — an enormous mass of intrusive **igneous** rock—rock made of once-molten material—that has solidified below the earth's surface.

bedrock — general term for the solid rock that underlies soil and other material on the surface of the earth.

biodiversity — the full array of living things.

brackish — somewhat salty.

California Natural Diversity Database (CNDDB) — a statewide inventory of the locations and condition of the state's **rarest** plant and animal **taxa** and **vegetation types**. The CNDDB is a **natural heritage program** and is part of NatureServe's National Heritage Network, a nationwide network of similar programs.

California Wildlife Habitat Relationships System (CWHR) — an information system and predictive model for California's wildlife containing range maps and habitat relationships information on all of the state's regularly-occurring amphibians, reptiles, birds, and mammals.

canopy — defined here as the cover provided by a layer of vegetation, such as overstory trees in a forest.

carbonate — defined here as rock composed of carbonate minerals, especially limestone and dolomite.

catadromous — refers to **species** in which adults reproduce in salt water and juveniles **migrate** to fresh water to rear.

competition — term used when two or more organisms have the potential for using the same resource. Competition may be between individuals of the same **species** or between two or more different species.

continental plate — a **tectonic plate** on which a continent floats.

conservation — the use of natural resources in ways such that they may remain **viable** for future generations. Compare with **preservation**.

conservation easement — a purchased claim to some rights, generally development rights, on private property as a way of conserving both natural resources and private ownership.

crustaceans — a **taxonomic group** which includes crayfish and shrimp.

detritus — particles of organic material in various stages of decay.

distribution — defined here as the pattern of occurrences for a **species** or **habitat** throughout the state; generally more precise than **range**.

Ecological Reserve — designation given to certain lands owned or managed by the Department of Fish and Game as a way of regulating appropriate use. This designation is usually reserved for land with **special status** plants, animals or **vegetation types**. Compare with **Wildlife Area**.

ecosystem — a natural unit defined by both its living and non-living components; a balanced system for the exchange of nutrients and energy. Compare with **habitat** and **vegetation type**.

endangered - one of several **special status** listing designations of plant and animal **taxa**. Under the California and federal Endangered Species Acts, endangered refers to a **taxon** that is in danger of becoming **extinct** throughout all or a significant portion of its **range**. The word endangered is also commonly applied to non-listed **taxa** in danger of extinction.

endemic — found only in a specified geographic region.

endemism — used here as a measure of **distribution** for those **taxa** that are found only in one specific area, such as one region or the state itself. A region of high endemism has many taxa restricted to it.

estuary — an area in which salt water from the ocean mixes with flowing fresh water, usually at the wide mouth of a river.

evolutionarily significant unit (ESU) — refers to a genetically distinct population segment of a **species**. An ESU is protected under the federal Endangered Species Act, which defines species to include "any subspecies of fish or wildlife or plants, and any distinct population segment of any species of vertebrate fish or wildlife which interbreeds when mature."

extant — still existing.

extinct — refers to a plant or animal or **vegetation type** that no longer exists anywhere.

extirpated — refers to a plant or animal or **vegetation type** that has been locally eliminated, but is not **extinct**.

fauna — refers to all of the animal **taxa** in a given area.

flora — refers to all of the plant **taxa** in a given area.

forb — a broad-leaved herb, such as clover, as distinguished from a grass or a woody plant.

genus — the level of biological classification above **species**. Many species can belong to the same genus.

geographic information system (GIS) — an organized assembly of people, data, techniques, computers, and programs for acquiring, analyzing, storing, retrieving, and displaying spatial information about the real world.

habitat — where a given plant or animal **species** meets its requirements for food, cover, and water in both space and time; may or may not coincide with a single **vegetation type**.

home range — the area in which an individual animal travels in the scope of normal activities; not to be confused with **range** or **distribution**, which refer to entire **taxa**.

hybridization — refers here to the crossbreeding of two animals or plants of different species or subspecies.

igneous — refers here to rock that is formed by solidification of molten material (magma) from within the earth.

introduced — refers to any **species** intentionally or accidentally transported and released into an environment outside its **native** range.

invasive — an **introduced species** which spreads rapidly once established and has the potential to cause environmental or economic harm. Not all introduced species are invasive.

invertebrate — an animal without an internal skeleton. Examples are insects, spiders, clams, shrimp, and snails.

latitude — an imaginary horizontal line representing degrees north or south of the Equator. The Equator is zero degrees while the North Pole is 90 degrees north.

listed — general term used for a **taxon** protected under the federal Endangered Species Act, the California Endangered Species Act, or the California Native Plant Protection Act.

longitude — an imaginary vertical line representing degrees east or west of the Prime Meridian at Greenwich, London. Greenwich is zero degrees while the line directly opposite it (in the Pacific Ocean) is 180 degrees west or east of the Prime Meridian.

migratory — refers to animals which travel seasonally. Migrations may be local or over long distances.

mollusks — a **taxonomic group** of **invertebrate** organisms which includes clams, mussels, snails, and slugs.

monitoring — collecting and analyzing observations of a **species, habitat**, or **vegetation type** over time. Monitoring also includes collecting data on other **ecosystem** components such as water and soil.

native — naturally-occurring in a specified geographic region.

natural community — general term often used synonymously with **habitat** or **vegetation type**.

natural heritage program — a member program in a network under NatureServe. These programs gather, manage, and distribute detailed information about the biological diversity found within their jurisdictions. Most United States natural heritage programs are within state government agencies, while others are within universities or field offices of The Nature Conservancy.

non-vascular plant — a plant without specialized tissues for conducting water and nutrients. Mosses are one example.

olfactory — of the sense of smell.

Pacific Flyway — the westernmost migratory bird flyway in North America, which begins in Alaska and runs south through California. It consists of several parallel routes linked together by several branches and follows the coast of North America and the valleys of the major mountain ranges.

plant alliance — a level of classification for **vegetation types** generally based upon the dominant plant **species** in the uppermost or dominant layer of vegetation.

plant association — a level of classification for **vegetation types** below **plant alliance** and defined by the most characteristic species associated with a plant alliance. Many plant associations may be nested within a single plant alliance just like many **species** may be nested within a single **genus**.

population — the number of individuals of a particular **taxon** in a defined area; not to be confused with **species richness**.

predation — the act of killing and eating other animals.

preservation — generally, the non-use of natural resources. Compare with **conservation**.

quad — defined here as a 7.5 minute quadrangle published by the United States Geological Survey (USGS) at a **scale** of 1:24,000.

range — defined here as the maximum geographic extent of a **taxon** or **habitat**; does not imply suitable conditions exist throughout the defined limits. Compare with **distribution**.

rare — one of several **special status** listing designations in state law; it applies only to plants. Under California law, a plant is rare when, although it is not in immediate danger of extinction, it occurs in such low numbers that it may become **endangered** if its environment worsens. The word rare is also commonly applied to non-listed plants and animals whose populations are low in number and therefore at risk.

rarity — used here as a measure of sensitivity for those **taxa** that have special status due to very limited **distribution**, low population levels, or immediate threat. An area high in rarity has many taxa that meet this definition.

resident — refers to animal **taxa** which remain in a given location throughout the year.

richness — used here as a measure of diversity. It is the total number of plant **taxa**, animal species, or **vegetation types** in a given area.

riparian — of or relating to rivers or streams.

salmonids — collective term for a family of fish that includes salmon and trout.

scale — defined here as the relationship between distance on a map and distance on the surface of the earth. Scale may be expressed with distance units (e.g., 1 inch = 200 feet) or without distance units (e.g., 1:24,000).

special status — collective term for all categories of plant or animal **taxa** whose **populations** are **rare** and at risk. The **CNDDB** tracks special status taxa, which meet one or more of the following criteria:

Is **listed,** is a candidate for listing, or is proposed for listing under the California or federal Endangered Species Acts or California Native Plant Protection Act as **Endangered**, **Threatened,** or (for plants only) **Rare**;

Is a federal "Species of Concern," an unofficial designation sometimes seen on USFWS species lists;

Meets the criteria for listing, even if not currently included on any list, as described in Section 15380 of the California Environmental Quality Act (CEQA) Guidelines;

Has been designated as a special status, sensitive, or declining taxon by other state or federal agencies or non-governmental organizations, including Bureau of Land Management and U.S. Forest Service;

If an animal, is considered by DFG to be a **Species of Special Concern**;

If a plant, is listed in the California Native Plant Society's *Inventory of Rare and Endangered Plants of California* (CNPS 2001);

Is biologically rare, very restricted in **distribution**, declining throughout its **range**, or has a critical, vulnerable stage in its life cycle that warrants monitoring;

Has **population**(s) in California that may be peripheral to the major portion of its range but is threatened with **extirpation** in California; or

Is closely associated with a **habitat** that is declining in California at a significant rate (*e.g.,* **wetlands**, **riparian** habitats, old growth forests, desert aquatic systems, native grasslands).

speciation — the process by which new **taxa** evolve**.**

species — the highest level of biological classification from which organisms can breed and produce fertile offspring under natural conditions.

Species of Special Concern — an administrative designation given to animals that are not **listed** under the federal Endangered Species Act or the California Endangered Species Act, but are declining at a rate that could result in listing.

subspecies — the level of biological classification below **species**; a genetically-distinct group.

taxa — a term used to refer collectively to organisms at different levels of biological classification. For example, **species, subspecies, varieties, and evolutionarily significant units (ESUs)** together may be referred to as taxa.

taxon — the name that is applied to a group in biological classification, for example, **species, subspecies, variety, or evolutionarily significant unit (ESU)**. The plural is **taxa.**

taxonomic group — used here to refer to organisms at the same level of organization in biological classification, for example, kingdom, phylum, class, or order.

tectonic plate — one of the many large plates which make up the crust of the earth and move slowly around it, sometimes colliding with or pulling apart from other plates.

temperate — used here to describe climates neither extremely hot nor extremely cold.

terrestrial — growing, living on, or frequenting land.

threatened — one of several **special status** listing designations of plant and animal **taxa.** Under the California and federal Endangered Species Acts, threatened refers to a **taxon** that is likely to become **endangered** in the foreseeable future. The word threatened is also commonly applied to non-listed taxa in danger of extinction.

Tertiary Period — the period in geologic history from about 50 million years ago to about 2.7 million years ago.

topography — the shape of the surface of the earth, including mountains and valleys.

upland — a general term referring to **species, habitats,** or **vegetation types** in non-flooded or non-saturated areas.

vagrant — an animal, usually **migratory**, straying outside of the normal **range** for its species. Many vagrants occur in California because of the state's large size; diverse **habitats** and **topography**; proximity to the ocean, where storms originate; long coastline and large marine area; and nearness to Canada, Asia, and Mexico.

vascular plant — a plant with specialized tissues for conducting water and nutrients. Examples are ferns and wildflowers.

vegetation type — a natural unit similar in definition to **ecosystem**, but defined primarily by the composition of plant **species**; compare also with **habitat**.

vernal pools — seasonal **wetlands** that form in depressions on the soil surface above a water-restricting layer of soil or rock. Plant and animal **taxa endemic** to vernal pools are those which can adapt to a unique cycle of flooding, temporary ponding, and drying.

vertebrate — an animal with an internal skeleton. Examples are birds, mammals, reptiles, amphibians, and fish.

viable — able to persist over time; self-sustaining.

watershed — defined here as a stream or river basin and the adjacent hills and peaks which "shed," or drain, water into it.

wetland — a general term referring to the transitional zone between **aquatic** and **upland** areas. Some wetlands are flooded or saturated only during certain seasons of the year. **Vernal pools** are one example of a seasonal wetland.

wildlands — collective term for public or private lands largely undeveloped and in their natural state.

Wildlife Area — designation given to certain lands owned or managed by the Department of Fish and Game as a way of regulating appropriate use. This designation is usually given to land with potential for multiple wildlife dependent public uses such as waterfowl hunting, fishing, or wildlife viewing. Compare with **Ecological Reserve**.

xeric — dry or desert-like.

zooplankton — minute, often microscopic, animal life that drift or swim in water bodies such as the ocean.

References

Metadata for GIS coverages may be found online at
atlas.dfg.ca.gov

Abbott, I. and G. J. Hollenberg. 1976. *Marine Algae of California.* Stanford University Press. Palo Alto, California.

Alt, D. D. 2000. *Roadside Geology of Central and Southern California.* Mountain Press Publishing. Missoula, Montana.

Alt, D. D. and D. W. Hyndman. 1975. *Roadside Geology of Northern California.* Mountain Press Publishing. Missoula, Montana.

American Fisheries Society. 1991. *Common and Scientific Names of Fishes from the United States and Canada.* Fifth Edition. American Fisheries Society Special Publication 20. Bethesda, Maryland.

American Ornithologists' Union. 1998. *The A.O.U. Checklist of North American Birds.* Seventh Edition. American Ornithologists' Union. Washington, D.C.

Bradford, D. F. 1992. "Biogeography and endemism in the Central Valley of California." In: Williams, D. F., S. Byrne, and T. E. Rado (editors). *Endangered and Sensitive Species of the San Joaquin Valley, California: Their Biology, Management and Conservation.* Published by the California Energy Commission based on a conference held at California State University, Bakersfield, December 1987. Sacramento, California.

California Department of Conservation (CDC). 2001. *Important Farmland (Agricultural Land Use).* GIS coverages. Division of Land Resource Protection, Farmland Mapping and Monitoring Program. Sacramento, California.

California Department of Conservation (CDC). 2002. *Serpentine: California State Rock.* California Geological Survey. Note 14. *www.consrv.ca.gov/CGS/information/ publications/cgs_notes/index.htm*

CALFED Bay-Delta Program. 2002. *Ecosystem Restoration Program: Summer 2002 Report.* Sacramento, California.

California Department of Finance (CDOF). 2001. *Interim County Population Projections.* Sacramento, California.

California Department of Fish and Game (CDFG). 1996. *Great Valley Vernal Pool Distribution.* GIS coverage. Wildlife and Habitat Data Analysis Branch. Sacramento, California.

California Department of Fish and Game (CDFG). 1998a. *California Vernal Pool Assessment Preliminary Report.* Wildlife and Habitat Data Analysis Branch. Sacramento, California.

California Department of Fish and Game (CDFG). 1998b. *Distribution of Mitten Crab Sightings.* GIS coverage. Central Valley Bay Delta Branch and Wildlife and Habitat Data Analysis Branch. Sacramento, California.

California Department of Fish and Game (CDFG). 1999. *Kelp Bed Aerial Survey Data.* GIS coverage. Information Technology Branch and Marine Region. Sacramento, California.

California Department of Fish and Game (CDFG). 2001. *Red Fox Range.* GIS coverage. Habitat Conservation Planning Branch. Sacramento, California.

California Department of Fish and Game (CDFG). 2002a. *California Climate Based on the Köppen Classification System.* GIS coverage. Wildlife and Habitat Data Analysis Branch. Sacramento, California.

California Department of Fish and Game (CDFG). 2002b. *Anadromous Salmonid Ranges.* GIS coverage. Wildlife and Habitat Data Analysis Branch. Sacramento, California.

California Department of Fish and Game (CDFG). 2002c. *Native Trout Ranges.* GIS coverage. Wildlife and Inland Fisheries Division. Sacramento, California.

California Department of Fish and Game (CDFG). 2002d. *Central Valley Habitat Joint Venture Wetlands Projects.* GIS coverage. Wildlife Conservation Board. Sacramento, California.

California Department of Fish and Game (CDFG). 2003a. *California Natural Diversity Database.* Wildlife and Habitat Data Analysis Branch. Sacramento, California.

California Department of Fish and Game (CDFG). 2003b. *DFG Lands.* GIS coverage. Lands and Facilities Branch. Sacramento, California.

California Department of Fish and Game (CDFG). 2003c. *Conservation Planning Areas.* GIS coverage. Wildlife and Habitat Data Analysis Branch and Habitat Conservation Planning Branch. Sacramento, California.

California Department of Fish and Game (CDFG) and California Interagency Wildlife Task Group (CIWTG). 2002. *California Wildlife Habitat Relationships System.* Wildlife and Habitat Data Analysis Branch. Sacramento, California.

California Department of Fish and Game, National Oceanic and Atmospheric Administration Fisheries, and Pacific States Marine Fisheries Commission. 2002. *California Habitat Restoration Project Database.* Pacific States Marine Fisheries Commission. Sacramento, California.

California Department of Food and Agriculture (CDFA). 1997. *Starthistle Infestation by Township.* GIS coverage. Sacramento, California.

California Department of Forestry and Fire Protection (CDF). 2002a. *Multi-source Land Cover Data.* GIS coverage. Sacramento, California.

California Department of Forestry and Fire Protection (CDF). 2002b. *Migrated Census Blocks.* GIS coverage. Sacramento, California.

California Native Plant Society (CNPS). 1997. *California's Wild Gardens: A Living Legacy.* P. M. Faber, Editor. Published by California Native Plant Society for the Department of Fish and Game. Sacramento, California.

California Native Plant Society (CNPS). 2001. *Inventory of Rare and Endangered Plants of California.* Sixth Edition. Rare Plant Scientific Advisory Committee, David P. Tibor, Convening Editor. Sacramento, California.

Critchfield, H. J. 1983. *General Climatology.* Fourth Edition. Prentice-Hall, Inc. Upper Saddle River, New Jersey.

DiTomaso, J. M., G. B. Kyser, S. B. Orloff, and S. F. Enloe. 2000. "Integrated strategies offer site-specific control of yellow starthistle." *California Agriculture* 54(6):30-36.

Dobkin, D. S., A. C. Rich, and W. H. Pyle. 1998. "Habitat and avifaunal recovery from livestock grazing in a riparian meadow system of the northwest Great Basin." *Conservation Biology* 12:209-221.

Ewing, R. A., N. Tosta, R. Tuazon, L. Huntsinger, R. Marose, K. Nielson, R. Motroni, and S. Turan. 1988. *California's Forest and Rangelands: Growing Conflict Over Changing Uses.* California Department of Forestry and Fire Protection. Sacramento, California.

Fox, L. J. 1989. *A Classification, Map, and Volume Estimate for the Coast Redwood Forest in California.* Final report to the Forest and Rangeland Resources Assessment Program. California Department of Forestry and Fire Protection. Sacramento, California.

Gaines, D. 1974. *The Nesting Riparian Avifauna of the Sacramento Valley, California and the Status of the Yellow-billed Cuckoo.* MS thesis. University of California, Davis. Davis, California.

Geographical Information Center, California State University, Chico. 2002. *Sacramento River Riparian Vegetation, 1999 Update.* GIS coverage. Chico, California.

Goudey, C. B. and D. W. Smith. 1994. *Ecological Units of California: Subsections.* GIS coverage. United States Forest Service Pacific Southwest Region. San Francisco, California.

Grossman, D. H., D. Faber-Langendoen, A. S. Weakley, M. Anderson, P. Bourgeron, R. Crawford, K. Goodin, S. Landaal, K. Metzler, K. D. Patterson, M. Pyne, M. Reid, and L. Sneddon. 1998. *International Classification of Ecological Communities: Terrestrial Vegetation of the United States. Volume I. The National Vegetation Classification System: Development, Status, and Applications.* The Nature Conservancy. Arlington, Virginia.

Hickman, J. C. (editor). 1993. *The Jepson Manual: Higher Plants of California.* University of California Press. Berkeley and Los Angeles, California.

Huenneke, L. F. 1989. "Distribution and regional patterns of Californian grasslands." In: Huenneke, L. F. and H. Mooney (editors). *Grassland Structure and Function: California Annual Grassland.* Kluwer Academic Publishers, The Netherlands.

Jepson Flora Project. 2002. *Online Interchange for California Floristics.* Jepson Herbarium. Berkeley, California.

Jones, C., R. S. Hoffman, D. W. Rice, M. D. Engstrom, R. D. Bradley, D. J. Schmidly, C. A. Jones, and R. J. Baker. 1997. "Revised checklist of North American mammals north of Mexico, 1997." *Occasional Papers: Museum of Texas Tech University* 173:1-19.

Katibah, E. F. 1984. "A brief history of riparian forests in the Central Valley of California." In: R.E. Warner and K. M. Hendrix (editors). *California Riparian Systems: Ecology, Conservation and Productive Management.* University of California Press Ltd. London, England.

Knopf, F. L. 1995. "Declining grassland birds." In: LaRoe, E. T., G. S. Farris, C. E. Puckett, P. D. Doran, and M. J. Mac (editors). *Our Living Resources: A Report to the Nation on the Distribution, Abundance, and Health of U.S. Plants, Animals, and Ecosystems*. United States Department of the Interior, National Biological Service. Washington, D.C.

Knopf, F. L., R. R. Johnson, T. Rich, F. B. Samson, and R. C. Szaro. 1988. "Conservation of riparian ecosystems in the United States." *Wilson Bulletin* 100:272-284.

Lewis, J.C., K.L. Sallee, and R.T. Golightly, Jr. 1993. *Introduced Red Fox in California*. Final report to the Nongame Bird and Mammal Section, Wildlife Management Division. California Department of Fish and Game. Sacramento, California.

Manley, P. and C. Davidson. 1993. *A Risk Analysis of Neotropical Migrant Birds in California*. United States Forest Service report, Region 5. San Francisco, California.

Miles, S. R. and C. B. Goudey (compilers). 1997. *Ecological Subregions of California: Section and Subsection Descriptions*. Report #R5-EM-TP-005. United States Forest Service Pacific Southwest Region. San Francisco, California.

Miller, A. H. 1951. "An analysis of the distribution of the birds of California." *University of California Publications in Zoology* 50:531-643.

Moyle, P. B. 2002. *Inland Fishes of California*. University of California Press. Berkeley and Los Angeles, California.

Moyle, P. B., P. Randall, and M. Byrne. 1998. *Fish Distributions*. GIS coverages. University of California, Davis. Department of Wildlife, Fisheries and Conservation Biology. Davis, California.

Moyle, P. B. and L. H. Davis. 2000. "A list of freshwater, anadromous, and euryhaline fishes of California." *California Fish and Game* 86(4):246-258.

National Climatic Data Center. 2002. *Weather Observation Station Records*. Asheville, North Carolina. *lwf.ncdc.noaa.gov/oa/ncdc.html*

Pitcairn, M. J., R. A. O'Connell, and J. M. Gendron. 1998. "Yellow starthistle: survey of statewide distribution." In: Woods, D. M. (editor). *Biological Control Program 1997 Summary*. California Department of Food and Agriculture, Plant Health and Pest Prevention Services. Sacramento, California.

Saab, V. A., C. E. Bock, T. D. Rich, and D. S. Dobkin. 1995. "Livestock grazing effects on migratory landbirds in western North America. In: Martin, T. E. and D. M. Finch (editors). *Ecology and Management of Neotropical Migratory Birds: A Synthesis and Review of Critical Issues*. Oxford University Press, Inc. New York, New York.

San Francisco Estuary Institute. 1998. *Bay Area EcoAtlas: Wetlands and Related Habitats of the Bay Area*. GIS coverage. Oakland, California. *www.ecoatlas.org*

Spence, M.H. and D. White. 1992. *EMAP Sampling Grid Technical Report*. ManTech Environmental Technology, Inc. and United States Environmental Protection Agency Environmental Research Laboratory. Corvallis, Oregon.

Stebbins, R. C. 1985. *A Field Guide to Western Reptiles and Amphibians*. Second Edition. Houghton Mifflin Company. Boston, Massachusetts.

Stein, B. A., L. S. Kutner, and J. S. Adams. 2000. *Precious Heritage: The Status of Biodiversity in the United States*. The Nature Conservancy and Association for Biodiversity Information. Oxford University Press, Inc. New York, New York.

The Climate Source. 1998a. *California Average Monthly and Annual Precipitation, 1961-1990*. Corvallis, Oregon.

The Climate Source. 1998b. *California Average Monthly and Annual Temperature, 1961-1990*. Corvallis, Oregon.

Thomas, K., J. Franklin, T. Keeler-Wolf and P. Stine. 2002. *Mojave Desert Ecosystem Program: Central Mojave Vegetation Mapping Project*. GIS coverage. United States Geological Survey, Biological Resources Division. Flagstaff, Arizona.

United States Census Bureau (USCB). 2001. *Census 2000 Redistricting Data (Public Law 94-171) Summary File*. Suitland, Maryland.

United States Fish and Wildlife Service (USFWS) and Stephen P. Teale Data Center (TDC). 1997. *National Wetlands Inventory*. Sacramento, California.

United States Geological Survey (USGS). 1999. *National Elevation Dataset*. GIS coverage. Reston, Virginia.

United States Geological Survey (USGS). 2002a. *National Atlas of the United States: Principal Aquifers of the 48 Conterminous United States*. GIS coverage. Reston, Virginia. *www.nationalatlas.gov*

United States Geological Survey (USGS). 2002b. *National Atlas of the United States: Geology of the Conterminous United States at 1:2,500,000 Scale — A Digital Representation of the 1974 P.B. King and H.M. Beikman Map.* GIS coverage. Reston, Virginia. *www.nationalatlas.gov*

United States Geological Survey (USGS), Stephen P. Teale Data Center (TDC), United States Environmental Protection Agency (USEPA), and California Department of Fish and Game (CDFG). 1996. *California Hydrography.* GIS coverage. Information Technology Branch. Sacramento, California.

University of California, Santa Barbara (UCSB). 1998. *California Gap Analysis Project: Land-cover for California.* GIS coverage. Santa Barbara, California.

Warner, R. E. and K. M. Hendrix (editors). 1984. *California Riparian Systems: Ecology, Conservation and Productive Management.* University of California Press Ltd. London, England.

White D., A. J. Kimerling, and W. S. Overton. 1992. "Cartographic and geometric components of a global sampling design for environmental monitoring." *Cartography and Geographic Information Systems* 19(1):5-22.

Williams, D. F., E. A. Cypher, P. A. Kelly, N. Norvell, S. E. Phillips, C. D. Johnson, G. W. Colliver, and K. J. Miller. 1997. *Recovery Plan for Upland Species of the San Joaquin Valley, California.* United States Fish and Wildlife Service. Portland, Oregon.

Wright, T. L. and T. C. Pierson. 1992. *Living with Volcanoes, The U. S. Geological Survey's Volcano Hazards Program.* United States Geological Survey Circular #1073. *vulcan.wr.usgs.gov/Vhp/C1073/framework.html*

About the Authors

Helen Birss is the program manager for the Fisheries Restoration Grant Program, coordinating with a team of over 30 grant managers dedicated to restoring salmonid habitat in coastal California.

Roxanne Bittman has been the lead botanist for the California Natural Diversity Database since 1986, coordinating information about the locations, status, and trends of the state's special status plants.

Esther Burkett is a wildlife biologist in the Species Conservation and Recovery Program and has worked on Marbled Murrelet issues for over 10 years.

Scott Clemons is a public land management specialist with the Wildlife Conservation Board and has managed the California Riparian Habitat Conservation Program since 1993, working on numerous riparian habitat conservation initiatives.

Larry Espinosa, a biologist in the Office of Spill Prevention and Response, works to assess the impacts of oil spills and to recommend the most effective cleanup methods to reduce injury to our natural marine resources.

Barrett Garrison is an environmental scientist in the Sacramento Valley-Central Sierra Region specializing in the habitat relationships and community ecology of birds and other wildlife in California's oak woodlands and forests.

Diana Hickson is a botanist in the Wildlife and Habitat Data Analysis Branch, working on vegetation mapping and habitat conservation initiatives. She previously represented DFG on the California Interagency Noxious Weeds Coordinating Committee and the Riparian Habitat Joint Venture.

Kathy Hieb is a marine biologist for the Central Valley-Bay Delta Branch. She is the project leader for the San Francisco Bay Study, which involves long term monitoring of fish, shrimp, and crab abundance and distribution in the San Francisco Estuary, including introduced species such as the mitten crab.

Kathy Hill is currently a fisheries biologist in the Sacramento Valley-Central Sierra Region who previously worked on reptile and amphibian issues for the Species Conservation and Recovery Program.

Marc Hoshovsky has worked on statewide conservation planning issues in California for 16 years as staff to DFG and, recently, on assignment to the California Resources Agency.

Kevin Hunting is a wildlife biologist in the Wildlife and Habitat Data Analysis Branch who has worked on grassland bird conservation issues for the past eight years.

Dr. Diana Jacobs is Deputy Director and Science Advisor to the Director and DFG lead for the CALFED Bay-Delta Program.

Ron Jurek is a wildlife biologist for the Species Conservation and Recovery Program. He works on invasive animal issues when he is not working on special status birds such as the California Condor, Bald Eagle, and Least Tern.

Eric Kauffman has worked as a geographer for the State of California for over 10 years and is now a research specialist with the Wildlife and Habitat Data Analysis Branch.

Dr. Todd Keeler-Wolf is the lead vegetation ecologist for the California Natural Diversity Database and a co-author of the Manual of California Vegetation.

Chuck Knutson is a fisheries biologist in the Wildlife and Inland Fisheries Division, who has spent 27 years working in inland, anadromous, and marine fisheries management programs.

Kari Lewis is a conservation biologist in the Lands and Facilities Branch, coordinating land acquisition of the Ecological Reserve System. She previously worked in the Wildlife and Habitat Data Analysis Branch, where she co-authored the DFG's Vernal Pool Assessment Preliminary Report.

Dr. Eric Loft leads the Resource Assessment Program. While with the Wildlife Programs Branch, he initiated the large and wide-ranging mammal species concept with his colleagues to highlight the importance of these species in conservation planning.

Darlene McGriff is the lead zoologist for the California Natural Diversity Database and has worked on special status animal issues for over 20 years.

Becky Miller is an environmental scientist for the Habitat Conservation Planning Branch. She formerly worked as the statewide non-game fish species recovery and conservation coordinator.

Monica Parisi is a wildlife biologist and has managed the California Wildlife Habitat Relationships System since 1998, supporting the use of this terrestrial vertebrate model in analyses for biodiversity conservation.

Steve Parmenter, an aquatic biologist with the Eastern Sierra and Inland Deserts Region, works for the recovery of native fishes in the Owens River, Death Valley, and Mojave River basins.

Joe Pisciotto is a fisheries biologist specializing in salmonids in the Native Anadromous Fish and Watershed Restoration Branch.

Gail Presley is a wildlife biologist who supervises the Conservation Planning Program in the Habitat Conservation Planning Branch.

Ronald Rempel is a Deputy Director and Chief of the Habitat Conservation Division.

Ronald Rogers, an environmental scientist for the Wildlife and Habitat Data Analysis Branch, has varied experience in fisheries research and management as well as wildlife and wildlife area management.

Janine Salwasser is the lead information system specialist for the Oregon Watershed Enhancement Board, where she is developing a statewide natural resource information system in partnership with other agencies and universities. She previously served as Chief of the Wildlife and Habitat Data Analysis Branch.

Melanie Weaver is a wildlife biologist in the Wildlife Programs Branch and has worked in waterfowl management since 1996.

Index

By Subject

amphibians
    California compared with United States 2-3
    endemism in 2
    names used 9
    rarity of 3, 29
    richness of 2, 28-29
Bay/Delta Region *16*, 24, 33, 36, 39, 42, 44, *56*, 58, *58*, 71, 72,
    74, 78, 88, *88*
birds
    California compared with United States 2-3
    in coast redwoods 52
    endemism in 2, 32
    in grasslands 60
    names used 9
    in oak woodlands 54
    rarity of 3, 33
    richness of 2, 32-35
    in riparian habitat 56, *86*
    See also waterfowl.
Carson River *18*, 64
Cascade Range 24, 58, 64, 76
Central Coast Region *18*, 34, *82*
Central Valley 12, 16, 24, 26, 30, 32, 34, 36, 38, 39, 40, 42, 47, 50,
    56, 58, 60-63, *62*, 64, 71, 72, 76, 78, 86
    See also Sacramento Valley Region, San Joaquin Valley
    Region.
chaparral habitat 18, 22, 28, 34, 38
climate
    of California 12, 14-15
    of Central Coast and South Coast Regions 34
    of Klamath/North Coast Region 28
    of Modoc and Sierra Regions 40
    of Mojave Desert 66
    and plants 24
    of Sacramento Valley and San Joaquin Valley Regions 36
    and vegetation 18
    See also Mediterranean climate.
Colorado Desert Region 30, 32, 34, 38, 39, *68*
Colorado River 33, 34, 66
coast, Coast Ranges. *See* Central Coast Region, Klamath/North
    Coast Region, South Coast Region.
conservation easements 82
conservation planning
    Habitat Conservation Planning 84
    Joint Ventures 86
    Natural Communities Conservation Planning 84
Death Valley 2, 12, *12*, 30, 32, 66, *68*
Delta. *See* Bay/Delta Region.
deserts. *See* Colorado Desert Region, Mojave Region.
Ecological Reserves *62*, 82, *82*
Eel River 50, *90*
endangered species 44, *44*, 47, 52, 68, 74, 76, 84
endemism
    in amphibians 2
    in birds 2, 32, 60
    California rank in United States 2

    described 4
    in freshwater fishes 2, 68
    in insects 44
    in mammals 2, 38, *38*
    in reptiles 2
    in vascular plants 2, 16, 24, 66
extinction 44, 50, 52
Fish and Game Commission 82
fish hatcheries 50
fishes, freshwater
    California compared with United States 2-3
    endemism in 2
    names used 9
    rarity of 3, 43
    richness of 2, 42-43
    See also pupfishes, salmonids, trout.
fishes, marine 4
fishing, recreational 48, 82
geographic information systems (GIS) 5-7, 9, 84
geology 16-17, 18, 24, 26, 62, 66
grassland habitat, grasslands 18, 19, 22, *22*, 34, 36, 38, 42,
    44, 47, 58, 60-61, 82, 83
habitats. *See* chaparral habitat, grassland habitat, kelp forests,
    oak woodlands, redwood forests, riparian habitat,
    vernal pool habitat, wetlands.
hunting 82
insects
    in oak woodlands 54
    richness of 44
invasive species
    animals 76-79, *76*, *78*
    plants 26, 74-75, *74*
invertebrates
    examples of 4, 44, *44*
    in kelp forests 48
    names used 9
    rarity of 44-45
    in wetlands 58
    See also insects.
kelp forests 47, 48-49
Kern River 47, 64
Klamath Mountains 24, 58
Klamath/North Coast Region *16*, *18*, *22*, 24, 28, 38, *50*, *90*
Klamath River 50
Lake Tahoe 40
land acquisition 82-83, 84
limestone 16, 17, 66
mammals
    California compared with United States 2-3
    endemism in 2, 38, *38*
    in grassland habitat 60
    marine, in kelp forests 48
    names used 9
    in oak woodlands 54
    rarity of 3, 39
    in redwood forests 52
    richness of 2, 38-39
    selected wide-ranging 40-41